YOUR WORLD DOESN'T HAVE TO STAY THIS SMALL

A Practical Guide to Rebuilding Your Life After Trauma — Even When You're Not Ready

BILL GASIAMIS

Disclaimer: This book is for educational purposes only. It does not provide medical, psychological, or mental health advice and is not a substitute for professional care. If you are experiencing persistent distress, suicidal thoughts, or feel unsafe, seek immediate support from local emergency services or a qualified health professional.

A catalogue record for this work is available from the National Library of Australia.

ISBN (paperback): 978-0-6459191-3-4
ISBN (ebook): 978-0-6459191-2-7

First edition: 2026
Epigraph and quotation permissions: [to be confirmed prior to publication]

Cover design: Bill Gasiamis
Edited by: Jennifer Tomscha
Printed In Australia
billgasiamis.com

Dedication

For the person rebuilding quietly—the one who keeps going, even when no one seems to be watching them.

You don’t have to be okay to take the next step.

You just have to take the next step.

Preface

When I find myself in a room delivering a presentation on post-traumatic growth, I often ask the people to raise their hands if they've heard about post-traumatic stress disorder. Most of the hands in the room always go up. But when I ask about post-traumatic growth, very few people raise their hands—if any.

That gap has always felt important.

Because it tells me something: we've become familiar with the language of what trauma can take from us, but far less familiar with the language of what people can build after trauma—without pretending their trauma was worth it, without forcing gratitude, and without rushing toward a finish line.

This book exists to make that second conversation easier to have.

I know this territory from the inside. Between 2012 and 2014 I had three brain haemorrhages, and the third put me on an operating table. I'll tell you that story properly in a few pages. What matters here is what I've done with the years since: more than 400 conversations on the Recovery After Stroke podcast, a first book, and one long attempt to understand what actually happens when people rebuild after something that changes everything. This book is the clearest answer I've found so far.

This second conversation about post-traumatic growth is not a miracle promise. Not a feel-good slogan. And definitely not a way to minimise what you've been through. Post-traumatic growth isn't about being happy that trauma happened. It's about recognising that after something hard—something that shakes your sense of safety, identity, relationships, or future—many people do rebuild. Sometimes in ways they didn't expect. Sometimes in ways they can't fully explain until they finally have the language for it.

The research behind post-traumatic growth has been developing for decades. But research doesn't help you much when you're sitting in the messy middle of it—when you're functional on the outside and overwhelmed on the inside, when you don't know how to explain what's happening to you, when you're tired of advice that skips over reality.

So this book was written with one goal: to give you a clear path through that middle.

You'll find simple explanations, practical steps, and short exercises you can actually do—especially on hard days. You'll also find a steady message repeated in different ways, because most people don't need more information. They need something that helps them take the next step without turning healing into a deadline.

If you're reading this because life changed and you didn't ask for it, I want you to know something early:

You're not behind.

You're not broken.

And you're not alone.

You're rebuilding.

Table of Contents

Introduction

If trauma has left you feeling like your life split into "before" and "after," you're not imagining it. That split is real. It can show up in your body, your relationships, your confidence, your motivation, and the way you interpret the future.

And it can leave you with a strange kind of confusion: You might look okay to other people, but you don't feel okay inside.

Or you might be 'better,' yet still feel stuck.

Or you might be functioning, but not really living.

This is the stage most people don't get a map for.

The early stage has a name. The crisis has a name. Even the diagnosis often has a name. But the rebuilding phase—where your nervous system is trying to find safety again, where your mind keeps replaying what happened, where you're trying to make sense of who you are now—often feels unnamed.

This book names that feeling.

And more importantly, this book guides you through it.

You might be wondering who I am to guide you through any of this.

Fair question. Here's my answer.

In February 2012, I was 37 years old and certain of who I was. I made money. I put a roof over my family's head. I didn't rely on anybody. Healthy, strong, tough, capable—that was the list, and I could tick every box.

Then a blood vessel in my brain started leaking, and I spent seven days in hospital finding out that none of those boxes were load-bearing.

I went home with a set of instructions: don't go back to work, don't drive, don't do anything strenuous. One sentence from a doctor, and the identity I'd spent decades building was suspended until further notice.

A month later, it happened again. The second bleed took things I didn't know could be taken. I couldn't start a sentence and land the ending. I couldn't type an email. My emotions went everywhere, mostly to anger. And here's the strangest part: I looked *fine*. People kept telling me how great I looked while I was disappearing inside.

My world got small, fast. We'd arrive at a party and leave early—or I'd quietly find the host's bedroom and sleep while the party carried on at full volume down the hall.

The doctors, I want to be clear, did their job. They patched me up and sent me home, and they did that part very well. But nobody had anything for what came after. Friends said "let me know if you need anything" and meant it, then never turned up. What I actually needed didn't seem to exist: a path forward. Proof. Somebody further down the road than me, turning around and saying *it leads somewhere.*

The hospital had put me on a drug called dexamethasone to reduce the swelling in my brain. It also gave me insatiable hunger, sleepless nights, hallucinations, and the sensation of ants crawling on my skin—which, given everything else, felt like overkill.

One morning—the kids at school, the house quiet—I sat alone at the kitchen table, opened my laptop, and typed: *how to reduce inflammation in your brain.*

That's it. That's the heroic origin story. A search bar.

But that search opened a door I've never stopped walking through. I changed what I ate. (I'd already quit smoking and drinking—the day of the first bleed, as it happens. Fear is an underrated motivator.) One small change created a little evidence that I wasn't helpless. Evidence created momentum. Momentum created the next step.

I want to be honest with you: the small steps didn't make me bulletproof. In November 2014, a third bleed put me into brain surgery — two weeks after my mother-in-law passed away. Life does not politely queue its disasters. I woke from that surgery unable to walk. It took a month of inpatient rehabilitation before I came home, and seven years before I returned to work in any meaningful sense. But somewhere in those years, something had changed. I wasn't waiting to feel ready anymore. I knew how to take the next step from wherever I was standing.

Eventually I started a podcast, partly to find the people I'd needed in 2012—the ones further down the road. More than 400 interviews later, I can tell you what they have in common.

They talk about solutions more than problems. They're busy helping other people. They're chasing purpose and meaning. They are, to use the research term, the epitome of post-traumatic growth.

Some of them don't even know it.

I didn't either. I'd finished writing my first book—*The Unexpected Way That a Stroke Became the Best Thing That Happened*—before I stumbled onto the research of Lawrence Calhoun and Richard Tedeschi, who had been studying this for decades and had given it a name: post-traumatic growth. The relief was enormous. I didn't have the words. They did.

Now—your hard thing probably isn't a stroke. It might be a divorce, a diagnosis, a redundancy, a business that went under, a loss, or a phone call that split your life into before and after. The details matter less than you'd think. I've watched this pattern in hundreds of people, and it isn't neurological. It's human.

This is the book I needed at that kitchen table. That's why it exists—and it's why it's built the way it's built.

Each chapter follows a simple rhythm: it starts with a moment you might recognise, then it explains what's actually happening beneath the surface, and then it gives you a small plan—something you can do, not just something you can understand.

You don't need to believe in big transformations to use this book. You don't need to be ready. You don't need to have the perfect mindset. You just need enough willingness to take one step—because one step creates evidence, and evidence creates momentum.

That's how growth begins. Not as a breakthrough. As a build.

So if you're not okay yet, you're in the right place.

Let's start.

Part One: Understanding the Aftermath

The first eight chapters are about understanding what happened to you — and why it affected you the way it did. This section won't fix anything. That's not its job. Its job is to give you language, clarity, and permission to stop fighting your own experience. If you're tempted to skip ahead, that's understandable. But the chapters in Part Two will land harder if Part One has done its work.

"There is no agony like bearing an untold story inside you."

— Zora Neale Hurston,
Dust Tracks on a Road (1942)

1

If You Feel Like No One Gets It

I know what it's like to feel like no one understands what you're going through.

Not because I want to make this about me, but because I've spent years listening to people describe the aftermath of a hard event in almost the exact same way—different stories, different losses, different timelines. But these people describ the same internal experience.

It's the part where you're functioning just enough to look 'okay' to the world, but inside you're not okay at all.

And that can mess with your head.

Because when you look fine on the outside, people assume you *are* fine. Then you start wondering if you're the problem.

You're not.

You're just in the part of the story that nobody prepared you for.

Lie #1: "If I'm Not Okay Yet, I'm Doing Recovery Wrong."

This is the thought that quietly poisons the early rebuilding stage:

If I'm not okay yet, I'm doing recovery wrong.

It sounds reasonable. It even sounds responsible—like you're holding yourself accountable.

But it turns healing into a deadline.

And deadlines create pressure.

Pressure creates shame.

Shame creates silence.

And silence is where people get stuck.

So let's do something right now that will save you months—maybe years—of unnecessary suffering.

Let's call that thought what it is:

A lie.

Not a malicious lie. More like a lazy one. A lie that shows up when your nervous system is tired and your brain is desperate for certainty.

What "Okay" Actually Means

A lot of people think okay means:

- I'm back to normal
- I don't feel sad anymore
- I don't think about it
- I'm fully confident
- I'm done with the hard part

But that's not 'okay.'

That's a fantasy.

Okay means something far more practical:

Okay means I can take the next step.

That's it.

Not the whole staircase.

Not the whole next year.

Not the full plan for the future.

Just the next step.

And if you can take the next step, you're not failing.

You're rebuilding.

Why This Feels So Hard (And Why It Makes Sense)

Here's what people don't tell you about the aftermath: the hardest part is often not the event itself.

It's what comes after it.

Because the after is where you realise you can't go back to who you were before.

The old version of life had an operating system you didn't even notice. Things made sense. You trusted the flow. You could assume tomorrow would behave roughly the way yesterday did.

Then something happens.

And now you're living in a different reality.

Even if the outside world looks the same, your inside world doesn't.

So of course you feel confused. Of course you feel tired. Of course your mood changes. Of course your motivation comes and goes. Of course you have moments where you think: What's wrong with me?

Nothing is wrong with you.

You're adapting.

And adaptation can look messy at the beginning.

The Enemy Has a Name: Confusion

If I had to name the main villain of this early stage, it would be confusion.

Confusion keeps you looping.

Confusion makes everything feel urgent, uncertain, and heavy at the same time.

Confusion says:

- "I don't know what I'm supposed to do."
- "I don't know who I am now."
- "I don't know if I'm getting better."
- "I don't know what this means about my future."

And when you don't know, you hesitate.

When you hesitate, you stall.

When you stall, you start believing you're stuck.

But stuck is not your identity.

Stuck is a stage.

We'll take confusion apart properly in Chapter 4. For now, it's enough to know its name.

How to Get Unstuck Without Faking It

This book is not about pretending something horrible was "good."

It's also not a motivational speech disguised as self-help.

Think of it more like this:

A guidebook for rebuilding.

And the plan is simple. Not easy—but simple.

Step 1: Stop Using "Fine" as the Goal

Because "fine" is vague. And vagueness is where confusion thrives.

Step 2: Replace "Fine" With "Next Step"

Because the next steps are real. Measurable. Doable.

Step 3: Build Proof That You're Moving

Because your brain needs evidence. Not pep talks.

That's the strategy.

Tiny proof, stacked over time, becomes confidence.

And confidence makes growth possible.

Try This Today: The "Okay = Next Step" Test

Take ten minutes. Set a timer if you need to.

Write this sentence at the top of a page:

"Okay means I can take the next step."

Now answer these questions honestly:

1. What's one thing I'm trying to rush?

---

2. What's one thing I can do today that counts as a next step?

(Keep it small. Almost annoyingly small.)

---

3. What would I stop doing if I stopped treating healing like a deadline?

Now pick your next step and do it within 24 hours.

Not because it fixes everything.

Because it proves something:

You're not trapped.

What This Book Is (And What It's Not)

I need to be clear about something, because this topic attracts a lot of fluff.

This book is not here to diagnose you.

It's not here to give you a perfect mindset or help you to achieve a particular goal.

And it's definitely not here to pressure you into finding meaning before you're ready.

This book is here to do what I've always loved doing: simplify complicated ideas, make them practical, and help you take action in a way that actually sticks.

It will introduce you to post-traumatic growth in a grounded way—based on the foundational work that emerged in the 1990s and has expanded since—without turning your pain into a lecture.

And it will give you tools that you can test, keep, and make your own.

If You Do Nothing, Here's What Happens

If you keep treating healing like a finish line, you'll keep failing yourself on the days you need compassion the most.

You'll start hiding how you really feel.

You'll stop asking for support.

You'll assume you're behind.

And you'll carry unnecessary shame on top of the pain you're already working through.

That's not strength.

That's extra suffering.

If You Take the Next Step, Here's What Becomes Possible

If you switch your desire to be "okay" into a desire to do the "next step," something changes.

You stop demanding an outcome and start building momentum.

You stop measuring yourself against the old you.

You start becoming the you who can carry this.

And eventually—without forcing it—something else begins to show up:

Hope.

Not hype.

Not fake positivity.

Real hope. The kind that comes from evidence.

The kind that says:

"This isn't the end of me."

And that's what we're doing here.

We're not rushing you to a bright future, where you don't think about your past and about what happened to you.

Instead, we're helping you take the next step—until the next step becomes its own path.

"Give sorrow words: the grief that does not speak / Whispers the o'er-fraught heart and bids it break."

— William Shakespeare, *Macbeth* **(c. 1606)**

2

The Secret Wish Nobody Says Out Loud

Most people don't actually want growth after trauma.

They want their old life back.

They want to rewind the tape and return to the version of themselves who didn't have this chapter. The body that felt dependable. The mind that didn't scan for danger. The future that felt predictable. The simple confidence of waking up and assuming the day would behave.

And when that doesn't happen—when you can't go back—something strange kicks in.

You start living in a constant comparison.

"I used to be able to..."

"I never used to feel like this..."

"Why can't I just get back to normal?"

If you're doing that, you're not broken.

You're grieving.

The Real Problem: You Can't Go Back to Who You Were

Here's the truth most people avoid because it hurts:

You can't go back to who you were.

Not fully. Not exactly. Not in the way you mean it when you say *back*.

And this is where people get stuck—not because they're weak, but because they keep trying to build their life on an old blueprint.

The old blueprint was written for a life where this didn't happen.

So every time you try to force yourself into the old plan, reality pushes back.

That pushback feels like failure.

But it's not failure.

It's a mismatch.

Lie #2: "Going Back Is the Goal"

The lie is subtle. It sounds like hope. It sounds like motivation.

"Once I'm back to normal, I'll be okay."

But "back to normal" becomes a moving target. A finish line that keeps shifting. And the more you chase it, the more you feel like you're losing.

Because normal was built on assumptions you didn't even know you had.

And trauma has a way of cracking those assumptions.

The Way Forward Isn't Restoration – It's Reconstruction

Here's the reframe that changes everything:

The way forward isn't restoration.

It's reconstruction.

Restoration says: "Put it back the way it was."

Reconstruction says: "Build something that fits now."

That doesn't mean you're happy this happened. It doesn't mean you approve of this trauma and its effects. It doesn't mean you're pretending the pain is a gift.

It means you stop negotiating with reality.

You stop using the past as the only acceptable option.

You start building from where you actually are.

What You're Really Grieving (Even If You Can't Name It)

A lot of people think grief is only about losing a person.

But grief is also about losing a version of life.

Sometimes what you're grieving is obvious—your health, your safety, your relationship, your home, your job, your sense of confidence.

But sometimes you're grieving things that were invisible before the trauma, like:

- certainty
- predictability
- trust
- ease
- spontaneity
- the assumption that tomorrow would behave like yesterday

And that grief can make you feel like you don't recognise yourself.

You're more cautious. More tired. More reactive. More flat. More angry. More sensitive.

Or you're the opposite—numb, detached, on autopilot.

And then you do the most human thing possible:

You judge yourself for it.

You tell yourself you should be stronger, better, faster, more grateful, less emotional.

But what you're actually experiencing is a normal response to a changed world.

Your old internal map doesn't match the territory anymore.

Why Trying to Go Back Keeps You Stuck

This is important, because it's where your energy has been leaking.

When you keep trying to go back, you end up doing three things that quietly trap you:

1) You keep comparing today to a past that no longer exists

And every comparison ends with you losing.

2) You keep waiting for a version of you that may never return

Which makes the present feel like a holding pattern.

3) You keep postponing the work of rebuilding

Because rebuilding feels like admitting the truth.

And the truth is hard:

Some things changed.

Some things are gone.

Some things will never be exactly the same.

That's not pessimism.

That's reality.

This Is the Part Nobody Tells You About

After something big changes your life, there's a strange period where you're not quite who you were — and not yet who you're becoming. You might look the same to people around you. You might sound mostly okay. But inside, something has shifted, and you haven't figured out what to do with that yet.

That's not a problem to solve. That's a process to move through.

Grief — for the version of your life that existed before, for the person you used to be, for the future you thought you were building — is a completely legitimate part of this. You don't have to skip it to get better. In fact, trying to skip grief usually just means carrying it longer.

So if you're in that space right now — between who you were and who you're becoming — this is the right place to be. Not because it's comfortable. Because it's honest.

And being honest is where rebuilding actually starts.

The Enemy: The Rewind Fantasy

Let's name the enemy in this chapter:

The rewind fantasy.

It's the quiet belief that recovery means getting the old life back — that if you just heal hard enough, the tape rewinds.

The rewind fantasy sounds like hope. It isn't.

It keeps you measuring every day against a life that no longer exists. And when today has to compete with a memory, today always loses.

It also does something sneakier: it makes progress feel like betrayal. As if building a new life means admitting the old one is gone.

Here's the truth: missing your old life is grief, and grief is healthy.

Auditioning for your old life is the trap.

You're allowed to grieve what was. You're not required to keep applying for a position that's been closed.

Say This to Yourself

If you need a line to borrow when the grief hits, use this:

"I can miss who I was… and still build who I'm becoming."

And reality is the starting point of every meaningful rebuild.

"The world breaks everyone and afterward many are strong at the broken places."

— **Ernest Hemingway,** *A Farewell to Arms* **(1929)**

3

"It Wasn't That Bad"... Until It Was

A lot of people don't get stuck because they're weak.

They get stuck because they keep telling themselves they're not *allowed* to be affected.

They say things like:

- "It wasn't that bad."
- "Other people have it worse."
- "I should be over this."
- "I don't even know if this counts as trauma."

And I understand why people do that. It often starts as an attempt to stay strong. To be reasonable. To not make a fuss. To keep moving.

But there's a hidden cost:

When you minimise what happened, you also minimise what you need.

And then you wonder why you're still not okay yet.

You Think You Don't Qualify

Here's the problem we need to name early, because it quietly blocks everything else:

You might be reading a book about trauma and growth while simultaneously thinking…

"Yeah, but I don't think I belong here."

Not because you're trying to be difficult.

Because you've been trained—by culture, by family, by work, by social media, by comparison—to believe trauma has a minimum entry requirement.

Like there's a sign at the door that says: "Only the worst stories allowed."

And if your story doesn't match the examples people usually talk about, you start treating your own experience like it doesn't deserve attention.

Which is ironic because the fact you're here usually means it *already* has your attention.

Lie #3: "Trauma Only Counts If It's Big-T Trauma"

This is the lie that keeps people silent:

"Trauma only counts if it's extreme, dramatic, obvious, or violent."

If it's not one of those, you tell yourself to harden up. Push through. Be grateful. Keep busy. Move on.

But the mind and body don't work like that.

You can't out-tough what your nervous system has already decided was overwhelming.

You can't logic yourself out of an impact that has already happened.

And you definitely can't heal what you refuse to acknowledge.

Trauma Is About Impact, Not Competition

Here's the reframe:

Trauma isn't a competition.

And it isn't a headline.

Trauma is about impact.

It's about what happened *and* what it did to you.

Sometimes the event is unmistakable—a sudden loss, an accident, an assault, a diagnosis, a natural disaster, a life-altering betrayal.

But sometimes the trauma is quieter.

It can be:

- a long season of chronic stress
- a relationship that slowly eroded your confidence
- a childhood environment where you never felt emotionally safe
- a workplace that kept you in fight-or-flight for years
- a medical experience that made your body feel unpredictable
- a moment that snapped your sense of safety or control

And because it's quieter, you don't give yourself permission to take this trauma seriously.

But your system takes it seriously anyway.

Your Brain Is Trying to Protect You

If you've been arguing with yourself about whether it counts, let me offer another way to see it.

Your brain doesn't sit around deciding whether your story is dramatic enough.

Your brain is doing something far more basic:

Your brain is scanning for danger.

Your brain is trying to prevent a repeat.

Your brain is trying to work out what the rules are now.

So you might notice things like:

- you're more on edge than you used to be
- you avoid certain places, people, conversations, memories
- you feel flat when you think you should feel something
- you overthink everything
- you don't sleep properly
- you go through periods of irritability, sadness, numbness, panic, or exhaustion

And then you judge yourself for it.

But those responses aren't proof that you're dramatic.

They're proof that your system is adapting.

The "after" doesn't always look like a breakdown.

Sometimes it looks like functioning... without feeling like yourself.

And that can be harder to explain—especially when the outside world looks normal.

A Note on Professional Support

This book is designed to be genuinely useful. It draws on established research, offers practical frameworks, and gives you tools you can use without a therapist in the room.

But it is not therapy. And for some people, therapy — or another form of professional support — is not optional.

Here's a way to think about the distinction: this book can help you understand what's happening, name it accurately, and take structured steps through your trauma. What this book cannot do is provide the relational safety, clinical assessment, or personalised treatment that a trained professional can offer.

If any of the following are true for you, please treat professional support as a primary resource, not an alternative:

You are experiencing thoughts of suicide or self-harm.

You are using substances to manage your emotional state.

You are unable to function in daily life for extended periods.

Your symptoms have not reduced at all after several months.

You are dealing with trauma involving ongoing abuse, legal proceedings, or complex grief.

You have been diagnosed with — or suspect you have — PTSD, a mood disorder, or another condition requiring clinical management.

None of these indicate failure. They indicate that the level of support required is higher than a book can provide.

If you are unsure whether you need professional support, that uncertainty is itself worth exploring with someone qualified to help you assess it. A general practitioner, psychologist, or counsellor is a reasonable first contact.

This book works best alongside a life that includes adequate support. You are worth it. .

The Trauma Comparison Game

This is the part that pretends to be humility, but often acts like avoidance.

The trauma comparison game sounds like:

- "I shouldn't complain, because someone else…"
- "I have no right to feel this way, because other people…"
- "I'm lucky compared to…"

And look—gratitude is good.

Perspective is healthy.

But if you use comparison to silence yourself, you're not gaining perspective.

You're abandoning yourself.

Because here's what happens when you keep playing the comparison game:

You delay support.

You delay honesty.

You delay rebuilding.

You delay your life.

And you end up carrying shame on top of pain.

That's not resilience.

That's extra suffering.

The Permission You Might Need to Hear

If you're someone who has been thinking, "Maybe I'm overreacting," I want you to hear this:

You don't need permission from your past to care for your present.

You don't need your story to be the worst to deserve support.

You don't need to qualify to rebuild.

If something happened and it changed the way you live, think, feel, or trust…

You belong here.

Stop Debating What Counts and Start Naming Impact

Here's a practical shift that helps immediately:

Stop asking, "Does this count as trauma?"

Start asking, "What did this change?"

Impact moves you into clarity.

Impact gives you something to work with.

Impact gives you a starting point for reconstruction.

Marcus's Story

Marcus was 41 when his marriage ended. Not explosively — quietly. His wife told him she hadn't felt present in the relationship for years. There was no affair, no dramatic incident, no single moment he could point to and say: that's when it broke. Just a slow withdrawal he hadn't fully registered until it was already over.

He spent the first six months telling himself he had no right to be as affected as he was. People go through divorces every day. People lose children. People survive wars. What was a quiet separation compared to any of that?

What he didn't recognise — until much later — was that the absence of a dramatic story didn't reduce the disruption. His identity, his sense of the future, his daily structure, the person he thought he was building a life with — all of that had changed. The scale of someone else's loss doesn't set a floor on yours.

Here's what that can look like in practice.

The Enemy: The Suffering Hierarchy

Let's name the enemy in this chapter:

The suffering hierarchy.

It's the invisible ranking system that says pain only counts if it's worse than someone else's.

"Other people have it harder."

"It's not like I went through a war."

"I shouldn't complain."

The suffering hierarchy sounds like humility. It isn't.

It's suppression with good manners.

Because while you're busy ranking your pain, you're not processing it. Comparison doesn't shrink the impact. It just delays the repair.

Here's the truth: your nervous system doesn't check the leaderboard before it responds. Impact is impact.

Someone else's broken leg doesn't heal your broken arm. And someone else's bigger trauma doesn't erase yours.

Try This Today: The Impact Test (10 Minutes)

Grab a pen and a page.

Write this at the top:

"The thing that happened (or the season I went through) was..."

____

Now answer these four questions in one or two sentences each. Keep it simple. No essays.

1. What did it change about my sense of safety or control?

____

____

2. What did it change about how I see myself?

____

____

3. What did it change about how I see other people or relationships?

____

____

4. What did it change about how I see the future?

____

____

Now write one final line:

"Given that impact, it makes sense that I feel..."

____

That last sentence is the point.

Not because we're trying to justify staying stuck.

Because we're trying to remove shame from the equation.

When shame drops, movement becomes possible.

Why This Works: You Can't Rebuild What You Won't Name

This exercise works because it turns vague suffering into something specific.

When suffering is vague, you can't work with it. You can only endure it.

But when you name impact, you can start rebuilding the area that took the hit.

Safety.

Identity.

Trust.

Future.

Those are rebuildable categories.

And once you know which category you're dealing with, you stop trying to fix everything and start taking the next step that actually fits.

What Happens If You Keep Minimising

If you keep telling yourself your trauma doesn't count, here's what tends to happen:

- you stay silent longer than you should
- you keep performing "fine"
- you keep carrying it alone
- you get stuck in confusion and self-doubt
- you miss support that could actually help
- and you start believing your pain is a personality flaw

It isn't.

It's a response.

And responses can change.

What Becomes Possible When You Take Impact Seriously

When you stop debating and start naming impact, something subtle but important happens:

You stop fighting yourself.

You stop trying to win an argument with your feelings.

You stop pretending your nervous system didn't get the memo.

And that's when rebuilding becomes realistic.

Because you're no longer trying to be tougher.

You're being smarter.

You're taking your reality seriously enough to work with it.

And that's where growth becomes possible—not forced growth, not inspirational-post growth–but the kind of steady change that shows up over time when you do the work of reconstruction.

Say This to Yourself

If you need a line to borrow when comparison tries to shut you down, use this:

"If this event changed me, it matters."

Not because you're making it bigger.

Because you're finally making it honest.

You Don't Need the Worst Story to Deserve the Next Step

If you've been waiting for permission to take your experience seriously, this is it.

You don't need a dramatic story to be allowed to rebuild.

You don't need to prove your pain.

You only need to tell the truth about impact.

Because once you tell the truth, you stop negotiating with reality.

And when you stop negotiating, you can finally do what this book is really about:

Take the next step.

"Life can only be understood backwards; but it must be lived forwards."

— Søren Kierkegaard (1843)

4

Confusion Is a Special Kind of Exhausting

Confusion is one of the most underrated forms of suffering.

Not because it's dramatic. It isn't.

Because it's constant.

Confusion is the kind of thing that makes you look fine while you quietly fall apart inside your own head.

You can be sitting in a room full of people and still feel like you're floating. You can be doing life and still feel like you're not actually in it. You can be talking and still feel like your words don't match what's happening inside you.

And the worst part?

Confusion steals your energy without giving you anything back.

Confusion Keeps You Looping Instead of Rebuilding

If Chapter 1 gave you permission, and Chapters 2 and 3 helped you stop arguing with reality and qualifying your pain, then Chapter 4 is about what usually happens next:

You hit the mental fog.

The fog that sounds like:

- "I don't know what I'm supposed to do."
- "I don't know who I am now."
- "I don't know if I'm getting better."
- "I don't know what this means for my future."
- "I don't know what I'm feeling."
- "I don't even know where to start."

And because you don't know where to start… you don't.

You wait.

You research.

You think.

You replay.

You plan.

You try to figure it out.

Then you end the day feeling more tired, not more clear.

That's the trap: confusion feels like processing, but often it's just looping.

The Enemy, Up Close: Confusion

You met this enemy briefly in Chapter 1. Now we take it apart.

Let's call it what it is.

Confusion is the enemy in this stage.

Not because you're weak.

Because confusion has a specific effect: it makes everything feel urgent and impossible at the same time.

When you're confused, your mind starts treating your whole life like one giant unsolved puzzle. It piles every question into one messy heap and says:

"Solve all of it before you move."

And that's how people stay stuck for months, sometimes years—waiting for the day they finally feel clear enough to begin.

Lie #4: "I Need Clarity Before I Take Action"

This is one of the most believable lies in recovery:

"Once I understand everything, I'll move forward."

Sounds sensible. Sounds mature. Sounds responsible.

But it's backwards.

Clarity doesn't usually come *before* action.

Clarity comes *from* action.

Not big actions. Not life-changing action.

Small, concrete, stabilising action.

Because your brain is not convinced by pep talks. Your brain is convinced by evidence.

And when you take a step, you create evidence.

Evidence creates confidence.

Confidence creates momentum.

Momentum reduces confusion.

Your Brain Is Trying to Create Safety

Here's what I want you to hear, because it can remove a lot of shame:

Confusion is often your mind trying to protect you.

After trauma, your system becomes more alert. It scans. It tries to predict. It tries to prevent a repeat. It tries to work out what the new rules are.

- That can look like:
- overthinking
- analysing
- replaying conversations
- anticipating worst-case scenarios
- trying to find the "right" decision
- avoiding decisions altogether
- going numb because feeling is too much

It's not a personality flaw.

It's your nervous system saying, "I don't want to get blindsided again."

So you're not crazy.

You're adapting.

The issue is that the adaptation can become a prison if it keeps you in loops instead of steps.

What Happens If You Stay in Confusion

If you stay in the loop, here's what usually happens:

- you get more tired
- you become more avoidant
- you start believing you're broken
- you isolate
- you delay support
- you shrink your life without realising it

Confusion doesn't always look like chaos.

Sometimes confusion looks like you're managing, while your world quietly gets smaller.

The Difference That Changes Everything: Looping vs. Rebuilding

Looping feels like this:

- same thoughts
- same questions
- same mental arguments

- same self-doubt
- same exhaustion

Rebuilding feels like this:

- one decision
- one action
- one small shift
- one moment of stability
- one piece of evidence that you're not trapped

Looping drains.

Rebuilding restores.

And you don't need to be free of confusion to rebuild.

You just need to stop letting confusion set the rules.

Turn Confusion Into Structure

Here's the plan for this stage:

Step 1: Get confusion out of your head

Because it multiplies in there.

Step 2: Sort it into three buckets

So your mind stops treating everything as equally urgent.

Step 3: Choose one next step

Not the best step. Not the perfect step. The next step.

That's how you beat confusion.

Not by thinking harder.

By structuring your thinking and moving anyway.

Try This Today: The 3-Column Clarity Exercise (10 Minutes)

Grab a pen and a page.

At the top, write:

"What I'm confused about is…"

Now list your confusion as short lines. No paragraphs.

- ______________________________
- ______________________________
- ______________________________
- ______________________________

Now draw three columns and label them:

1) What I know

2) What I don't know (and may never fully know)

3) What I can do next

Now take each confusion line and sort it.

Example:

If you wrote, "I'm confused about what this means for my future."

- **What I know:** My life has changed. Some things are uncertain.
- **What I don't know:** Exactly how everything will turn out.
- **What I can do next:** One step that supports future-me this week.

If you wrote, "I'm confused about whether I'm getting better."

- **What I know:** Progress isn't a straight line. I have ups and downs.
- **What I don't know:** A neat timeline that guarantees anything.
- **What I can do next:** Track one small indicator for seven days instead of judging myself daily.

Now—here's the most important part—circle one item in the "What I can do next" column and write:

"The smallest version of this step is..."

Then do that within 24 hours.

Smallest version. That's the rule.

Because the goal isn't to solve your life.

The goal is to prove you're moving.

Confusion Pretends to Be Wisdom

Let's be honest: confusion can also feel safe.

Because confusion delays commitment.

If you stay confused, you don't have to risk hope.

You don't have to risk trying.

You don't have to risk disappointment.

You don't have to risk being seen.

You don't have to risk change.

So if part of you is holding onto confusion, that doesn't make you bad.

It makes you cautious.

But you don't want caution to become your whole identity.

So we loosen the grip gently.

One step.

One proof.

One piece of movement.

What Becomes Possible When You Take One Step Anyway

When you take one small step even while confused, something changes.

Not necessarily your circumstances.

But *you*.

You stop feeling trapped.

You stop waiting for a perfect emotional day.

You start building evidence that you can carry this moment.

And that evidence becomes the foundation for the next step.

That's how people rebuild: not with clarity first, but with movement first.

Say This to Yourself

If you need a line to borrow when your mind starts demanding certainty, use this:

"I don't need the whole map. I just need to know the direction."

Or even simpler:

"Confusion isn't my identity. It's my stage."

Confusion Doesn't Get to Decide Your Future

You don't beat confusion by outsmarting it.

You beat confusion by refusing to let it stall your life.

You get the confusion onto paper. You sort it. You choose one next step. You do the smallest version. You create evidence. You build momentum.

That's rebuilding.

And rebuilding is how you get your life back—not the old life, but a life that fits again.

"No one ever told me that grief felt so like fear."

— **C. S. Lewis,** *A Grief Observed* **(1961)**

5

Forcing Yourself to Be Positive Is the Fastest Way to Feel Alone

People mean well.

That's the frustrating part.

They don't want to see you hurting, so they reach for the most common advice in the world:

- "Stay positive."
- "Look on the bright side."
- "Everything happens for a reason."
- "At least you're alive."
- "You're so strong."
- "Just don't think about it."

Sometimes that lands like a warm gesture.

But sometimes it lands like a quiet message that says: "Your truth is too heavy for me."

And when you're not okay yet, that message doesn't motivate you.

It isolates you.

Forced Positivity Turns Healing Into Performance

Here's the problem with "just be positive" after trauma:

It doesn't create healing.

It creates pressure.

Pressure to look okay.

Pressure to sound okay.

Pressure to *make other people comfortable.*

So you do what a lot of good people do:

You edit yourself.

You keep the conversation surface-level.

You hide the parts that feel messy.

You pretend the hard days aren't happening.

And then you end up doing recovery alone in your own head.

That's not strength.

You hide your suffering and you perform for others instead.

Lie #5: "If I'm Still Hurting, I'm Doing It Wrong"

This is the lie hiding under forced positivity:

"If I'm still hurting, I'm doing it wrong."

It sounds like accountability, but it's actually shame.

And shame is not a motivator.

Shame is a muzzle.

It stops you from telling the truth.

It stops you from asking for support.

It stops you from admitting what you need.

So instead of healing, you start performing.

Positivity Is Not the Same as Healing

Let's reframe this clearly:

Positivity is not the same as healing.

And forced positivity can actually slow healing down.

Because healing requires integration.

Healing requires reality to be processed, and not skipped.

If you jump straight to the bright side, you end up building a life on top of feelings you haven't been allowed to have.

And those feelings don't disappear.

They leak.

The Truth You Avoid Doesn't Vanish – It Leaks

If you avoid the truth long enough, it will show up somewhere else.

It might show up as:

- sleep problems
- irritation
- fatigue
- tension
- numbness
- anxiety
- emotional outbursts
- withdrawal from people
- a life that quietly gets smaller

This is why forced positivity backfires.

It turns your inner world into a pressure cooker.

And eventually, the lid blows.

So let me give you permission to hold two things at once:

You can be grateful *and* grieving.

You can be strong *and* struggling.

You can be improving *and* still have hard days.

You can be changing for the better still feel pain.

That's not a contradiction.

That's being human.

The Enemy: Positivity Used as Avoidance

Let's separate something important here, because I'm not anti-hope.

Hope is good.

Optimism can be healthy.

Gratitude can be stabilising.

The problem is when positivity becomes a way to avoid reality.

Because then positivity stops being medicine and starts being a mask.

And masks have a cost.

A mask might help you get through a meeting or a family gathering.

But if you live in it, you lose touch with yourself.

And growth can't happen when you're disconnected from your truth.

Replace Forced Positivity With Honest Steadiness

So what do you do instead?

You don't have to become negative.

You don't have to vent endlessly.

You don't have to turn your pain into an identity.

You do something far more useful:

You become honest and steady.

Honest means you tell the truth about what you feel without judging it.

Steady means you take the next step that supports your stability.

That's the whole move.

Not flashy.

Not inspirational-poster energy.

Just grounded progress.

Try This Today: The Two Truths Exercise (10 Minutes)

Grab a pen and a page and write two sentences.

1. The hard truth is…

Finish it honestly. No censoring.

____

____

2. The steady truth is…

Finish it realistically. Not shiny. Not forced. Just supportive and doable.

____

____

Here are examples, in case your mind goes blank:

- Hard truth: "I feel scared about the future."

  Steady truth: "I can take one step today that supports future-me."

- Hard truth: "I miss who I used to be."

  Steady truth: "I'm rebuilding who I am now."

- Hard truth: "I feel angry this happened."

  Steady truth: "Anger is allowed, and I still get to choose my next step."

When you do this, something changes inside you.

You stop forcing yourself into either denial or despair.

You create a third option:

Truth plus movement.

That's the sweet spot.

How to Respond When Someone Says "Just Be Positive"

Let's make this practical too, because this is a real-life problem.

If someone says, "Just be positive," you don't have to argue with them.

You can say something like:

- "I'm working on being steady. Positivity can come later."

- "I'm taking it step by step. That's what helps."
- "I appreciate you. I'm trying to be real right now."

Short. Calm. No drama.

That way you protect your process without starting a war.

What Happens If You Keep Performing

If you keep trying to "look okay" to keep everyone comfortable, here's what tends to happen:

- you get lonelier
- you feel more misunderstood
- you stop trusting people with the truth
- you delay support
- you end up carrying shame you don't deserve

Performance doesn't heal you.

It just makes you harder to find—even for yourself.

What Becomes Possible When You Get Real

When you shift from forced positivity to honest steadiness, you get something powerful: Relief.

Relief doesn't mean the pain is gone.

Relief means you're no longer fighting yourself.

And when you stop fighting yourself, you can start rebuilding for real.

That's where change becomes possible.

Not because you posted a quote.

Because you started living in truth.

Say This to Yourself

If you need a line to borrow when you feel pressure to perform recovery, use this:

"I'm not here to be inspiring. I'm here to be real."

Or this one:

"Today, my job isn't to feel better. My job is to keep moving."

Truth Is the Beginning of Growth

You don't have to rush to the bright side.

You don't have to find meaning on command.

And you don't have to pretend you're fine to be worthy of support.

The way through this isn't forced positivity.

It's honest steadiness.

Truth… plus the next step.

That's what rebuilding looks like.

And that's what makes growth possible.

"Things don't really get solved. They come together and they fall apart."

— **Pema Chödrön,** *When Things Fall Apart* **(1997)**

6

The Day Your Old Rules Stopped Working

One of the strangest parts of the aftermath isn't the pain.

It's the realisation that the old rules don't work anymore.

The things you used to tell yourself to get through a hard week don't land.

The pep talk that used to fire you up feels empty.

The logic that used to calm you down can't reach you.

And that's when people start thinking:

"What is wrong with me?"

Nothing is wrong with you.

Your foundations took a hit.

You're Trying to Live on Cracked Foundations

Before the hard thing happened, you were living with a set of assumptions you didn't even know you had.

They weren't written down.

They weren't spoken out loud.

They were just there.

Assumptions like:

- "The world is mostly safe."
- "People are generally trustworthy."
- "My body will do what it's supposed to do."
- "If I work hard, things will be okay."
- "Bad things happen to other people."

Then trauma happens, and the assumptions crack.

So you're not only dealing with an event.

You're dealing with the collapse of the invisible structure you were standing on.

That's why everything feels harder than it should feel.

Lie #6: "If I Were Stronger, This Wouldn't Shake Me"

Here's the lie that keeps people blaming themselves:

"If I were stronger, I'd handle this better."

But strength isn't the issue.

The issue is that your mind is trying to build a new map while you're still walking.

That's not a weakness.

That's a normal response to a world that no longer feels predictable.

Trauma Is an Earthquake, Not a Mood

Trauma is not just a bad feeling.

It's an earthquake.

An earthquake doesn't just knock over a few things on the surface. It shakes what everything is built on.

And after an earthquake, you don't snap out of it.

You assess the damage.

You stabilise.

You rebuild.

So if you're in the stage where you feel shaky, uncertain, or not quite yourself, it doesn't mean you're failing.

It means you're living in the rebuild.

Your Core Beliefs Took the Hit

You can think of your core beliefs like the infrastructure of your life.

You don't notice infrastructure when it's working.

You only notice it when it breaks.

After trauma, the beliefs that often take a hit are things like:

Safety

"Am I safe in the world?"

Trust

"Can I trust people?"

Control

"Do I have any influence over what happens to me?"

Identity

"Who am I now?"

Meaning

"Does life make sense?"

Future

"What does the future even look like now?"

If one of those gets shaken, confusion makes sense.

If several of them get shaken at once, it can feel like you can't trust your foundations anymore. .

Not because you're dramatic.

Because your internal operating system is being rewritten.

The Enemy: The Broken Story You Tell Yourself

When your foundations crack, your brain tries to explain it.

And if you're not careful, the explanation becomes the enemy.

The enemy story usually sounds like one of these:

- "I'm broken."
- "I'll never be the same."
- "I can't trust anyone."
- "The world isn't safe."
- "Nothing matters."
- "I'll never feel normal again."

Now, some of those might feel true at the moment.

But here's the issue:

If you turn a stage into an identity, you lock yourself inside it.

So we're not denying what you feel.

We're changing the story from "I'm broken" to "I'm rebuilding."

That one shift is huge.

Stabilise First, Then Rebuild

This is the plan for this stage:

Step 1: Stop trying to solve your whole life

Because that's what cracked foundations make you want to do.

Step 2: Identify the exact foundation that took the hit

If you don't name what is broken precisely, you have a vague feeling that everything is hard. *Everything* isn't hard, but some things are hard right now. What exactly is hard for you? Name it, and be specific.

Step 3: Build one stabilising belief and one stabilising action

Because stability creates groundwork, and groundwork creates clarity.

This isn't motivational.

It's structural.

You stabilise the shaky parts first.

Then you build from this groundwork.

Try This Today: The Foundation Audit (10 Minutes)

Grab a pen and write this at the top of a page:

"Since this happened, the belief that changed the most is…"

Now complete the sentences that hit hardest:

1. **"The world used to feel ________. Now it feels ________."**
2. **"I used to trust ________. Now I struggle to trust ________."**
3. **"I used to feel in control of ________. Now I feel powerless about ________."**
4. **"I used to think of myself as someone who ________. Now I feel like someone who ________."**

5. "I used to assume the future would be ________. Now it feels ________."

Now choose **one** of those and write a replacement belief that is:

- true enough to say out loud
- kind enough to reduce shame
- practical enough to guide action

Examples:

- "The world isn't always safe, but I can build safety in my choices and my support."
- "Not everyone is trustworthy, but some people are, and I can choose carefully."
- "I can't control everything, but I can control the next step."
- "I'm not the old me. I'm becoming someone new."
- "The future is uncertain, but it isn't finished."

Finally, write one action under it:

"The next step that supports this belief in the next 24 hours is..."

Do the smallest version.

That's the rule.

Why This Works: Evidence Beats Anxiety

Your brain doesn't calm down because you tell it to.

It calms down when you show it proof.

A small stabilising action is proof.

Proof tells your system:

"I'm not helpless."

And when helplessness drops even slightly, you get access to something powerful:

Agency.

Agency is the beginning of rebuilding.

What Happens If You Don't Stabilise

If you don't stabilise the foundations, you end up doing life on shaky ground.

You'll keep second-guessing yourself.

You'll keep scanning for danger.

You'll keep waiting for certainty that never arrives.

You'll keep feeling like you're not okay yet, in a way that turns into self-attack.

That's not a moral failure.

That's an engineering problem.

And engineering problems can be fixed.

What Becomes Possible When You Rebuild

When you stabilise and rebuild, you start noticing subtle shifts:

- you feel less reactive
- you make decisions with less fear
- you trust your judgement again
- you stop arguing with your emotions
- you take steps without needing to feel perfect first

This is where the "change for the better" part begins—not as a shiny transformation, but as a steady structural upgrade.

Not because you wanted this.

Because you refused to stay collapsed.

Say This to Yourself

When you find yourself–or those you love–going back to the broken story, borrow this instead:

"My foundations were shaken. That's why this feels hard. I'm rebuilding."

Or even shorter:

"Shaken isn't broken."

You Don't Need Meaning Yet – You Need Stability

You don't have to force meaning right now.

You don't have to make a neat story out of pain.

But you can start rebuilding the foundations that make life feel livable again.

Safety. Trust. Identity. Future.

One stabilising belief.

One stabilising action.

One next step.

That's how you rebuild after an earthquake.

And that's how growth becomes possible—without pretending you're fine.

"The past is never dead. It's not even past."

— **William Faulkner,** *Requiem for a Nun* **(1951)**

7

If Your Mind Keeps Replaying It, You're Not Crazy

If your mind keeps replaying what happened, I want you to hear this first:

You're not crazy.

You're not weak.

And you're not failing at healing.

You're in a very normal stage where your brain is trying to do its job—make sense of a world that no longer feels predictable.

The problem isn't that you're thinking.

The problem is that the thinking has turned into a loop.

And loops are exhausting.

Rumination Feels Like Processing, But It Can Keep You Stuck

Most people call it overthinking.

It sounds harmless, even a bit relatable.

But after trauma, rumination isn't just a quirky habit. It can become a mental treadmill: lots of effort, no movement.

You replay conversations.

You revisit decisions.

You run "what if" scenarios.

You imagine different outcomes.

You rewrite the past in your head.

You argue with yourself.

You try to find the moment where everything went wrong.

And the longer you do that, the more tired you become.

Which makes it harder to take real steps.

Which makes you feel more stuck.

Which makes you ruminate more.

That cycle can become its own trap.

Lie #7: "If I Think About It Long Enough, I'll Finally Solve It"

This is the lie rumination sells you:

"If I just keep thinking, I'll work it out."

And sometimes thinking *does* help. There's a kind of reflection that leads to insight.

But rumination isn't usually insight-driven.

It's safety-driven.

It's your brain trying to prevent a repeat by analysing every detail. It's your mind trying to create certainty in a world that has proven it can be uncertain.

That's why rumination feels urgent.

It feels like you're doing something important.

But often you're not solving.

You're scanning.

Your Mind Is Trying to Create Safety, Not Meaning

Here's the reframe that changes how you respond to your own mind:

Your brain isn't replaying the event to torture you.

It's replaying it to protect you.

It's asking:

"What did I miss?"

"What should I have seen earlier?"

"How do I make sure this never happens again?"

"How do I stay safe from this kind of pain?"

Those are survival questions.

And survival questions don't shut off just because you want them to.

So again: you're not broken.

Your protection system is just stuck in overdrive.

Two Types of Rumination

This distinction matters, because it gives you a way forward.

There are two kinds of rumination:

1) Intrusive rumination

This is the uninvited kind. The loop that barges into your mind at the worst times. It's repetitive, draining, and often comes with that "here we go again" feeling. You're not choosing this rumination. It's happening to you.

2) Deliberate reflection

This is the chosen kind. It's structured. It has boundaries. It's you sitting down to make sense of what happened in a safe way—journaling, talking with someone supportive, or thinking with a clear goal.

Intrusive rumination drains you.

Deliberate reflection can rebuild you.

The goal isn't to stop thinking.

The goal is to shift from intrusive loops to deliberate reflection.

The Enemy: The Mental Treadmill

Let's name the enemy here:

The mental treadmill.

It looks like motion.

But it doesn't move you forward.

It just burns energy.

And because it burns energy, this mental treadmill leaves you less able to do the things that actually help: sleep, connect, eat properly, move your body, ask for support, rebuild routines, and take the next steps.

So the treadmill becomes self-reinforcing.

You don't need to win against it.

You need a way to step off it.

What Happens If You Stay on the Treadmill

If you stay stuck in rumination, a few things tend to happen:

- you get more tired
- you become more avoidant
- you lose confidence in your judgement
- you feel less present in your life
- you start thinking you're broken
- you delay the steps that would actually help

You don't need that extra suffering.

You've been through enough.

Contain the Loop, Then Convert It

Here's the plan for this stage. Simple. Not easy, but simple:

Step 1: Notice the loop without arguing

Arguing with it usually feeds it.

Step 2: Contain it with a boundary

So the loop doesn't hijack your whole day.

Step 3: Convert it into one deliberate question

Because questions with structure create movement.

Step 4: Take one next step

Because action gives your brain proof.

That's how you work with rumination instead of being owned by it.

Try This Today: The "Loop-to-Lesson" Exercise (10 Minutes)

Grab a pen. Set a timer for ten minutes. Write this at the top:

"The loop I keep getting stuck in is…"

Now answer these three prompts:

1. "What is my brain trying to protect me from?"

(Keep it simple.)

____

____

2. "What is the one question worth asking that could actually help me today?"

(Not "Why did this happen?"—that's too big. Make it workable.)

Examples:

- "What do I need right now?"
- "What boundary would reduce my stress?"
- "Who is safe to talk to?"
- "What is one stabilising action I can take?"

____

____

3. "What is one next step I can take in the next 24 hours?"

The smallest version.

____

____

When the timer ends, stop writing.

That's important.

Because the point isn't to think forever.

The point is to give your thinking a container so it becomes useful.

A Simple Boundary That Helps Immediately: "Thinking Time"

If your mind is looping all day, try this experiment for one week:

Give your mind a scheduled time to think.

Ten minutes. Same time each day.

When the loop shows up outside that time, you say:

"Not now. I'll think about this during thinking time."

You're not denying the thought.

You're postponing it.

This does two things:

1. It reduces the constant hijacking.

2. It teaches your brain you're in charge of when you engage.

And yes—at first your brain will act like a toddler who's been told no.

That's normal.

Consistency is what teaches your brain.

What Becomes Possible When You Convert Rumination

When you convert rumination into deliberate reflection, you start experiencing a different kind of thinking.

Not frantic.

Not compulsive.

Useful.

You start getting small insights.

You start feeling more agency.

You start trusting yourself again.

And this is where post-traumatic growth begins to become realistic—not as a meaningful story, but as a gradual strengthening of your inner system.

You're not just surviving the loop.

You're learning to steer.

Say This to Yourself

If you need a line to borrow when the loop shows up, use this:

"My brain is trying to protect me. I can give it structure."

Or even simpler:

"Not a loop. A next step."

Your Mind Doesn't Need More Thinking – It Needs Proof

You don't heal by thinking perfectly.

You heal by taking steps that make you feel safe enough to live again.

Rumination is your mind searching for safety.

So the answer isn't to shame yourself for looping.

The answer is to build safety through structure… and through action.

Contain the loop. Convert it. Take the next step.

That's how you step off the treadmill.

And that's how you keep moving.

"When we are no longer able to change a situation, we are challenged to change ourselves."

— Viktor E. Frankl (1946/1959)

8

The Question That Changes Everything

For a while after trauma, the main question is usually some version of:

"Why did this happen to me?"

And that question makes sense.

Your mind reaches for logic. Yourheart reaches for fairness. Your nervous system reaches for safety. You are trying to put the world back into order.

But here's what nobody tells you:

If you stay in "Why me?" too long, it becomes a trap.

Not because that question is wrong to ask.

But because it has no clean answer.

And when a question has no clean answer, you can spend years paying for it with your energy.

"Why Me?" Keeps You Tied to the Event

"Why me?" can turn into a mental anchor.

You keep circling the event, trying to squeeze certainty out of something that might always feel unfair.

You measure life against an alternate reality where this didn't happen.

You negotiate with the past.

And the longer you negotiate with the past, the harder it is to build a future that fits.

Because the future isn't built by perfect explanations.

It's built by decisions.

Lie #8: "If I Can Just Understand It, I'll Be Free"

This is the lie hiding under the "Why me?" question:

"If I can just understand it, I'll be free."

Sometimes understanding helps. It can bring relief.

But complete understanding is not always available.

And if you make freedom dependent on an answer you might never get, you'll stay stuck in a waiting room.

So the question becomes:

What do you do when the "why" won't resolve?

The Turning Point Isn't an Answer – It's a Shift

Here's the reframe:

The turning point isn't when you finally get the perfect explanation.

The turning point is when you shift the question.

From:

"Why did this happen to me?"

To:

"What now?"

That's not denial.

That's agency.

"What now?" is the moment you stop demanding life make sense before you move.

You stop handing your future to a question that can't pay you back.

You begin rebuilding on purpose.

Your Brain Wants Closure, But Your Life Needs Direction

The mind loves closure.

It wants a neat ending. A reason. A moral. A rule it can follow to guarantee this never happens again.

But trauma doesn't always offer closure.

Sometimes the story stays messy.

Sometimes the ending is unsatisfying.

Sometimes the person who hurt you never apologises.

Sometimes the body doesn't return to normal.

Sometimes life doesn't explain itself.

And that's where the shift matters most.

Because even without closure, you can still have direction.

Direction is not a perfect story.

Direction is a chosen action.

Priya's Story

Priya had been asking *why* for almost two years after her son's diagnosis. Why him? Why now? Why their family? She'd read everything she could find, as if understanding it deeply enough would eventually produce an answer that made it bearable.

The shift in her thinking happened during an unremarkable Tuesday. She was waiting at the pharmacy, and she noticed she'd stopped reading her phone and started watching a young woman manage three children across the waiting room — efficiently, warmly, without appearing to notice she was doing anything remarkable. Priya thought: I want to be that calm again.

This wasn'ta resolution. She still didn't have an answer to *why*. But for the first time in two years, she'd asked a different question — one that had somewhere to go. She booked one appointment that week. Then another. Her question of why never got answered. The life she built after that Tuesday did not require it to be.

Here's what that can look like in practice.

Try This: The Question Shift (10 Minutes)

The shift isn't about pretending the "why" doesn't matter. It's about deciding that your life can't wait for an answer that may never fully arrive. "What now?" is how you give your future a shape without needing the past to make sense first.

You don't have to stop asking "why." That question is human and it deserves some space. But you don't have to live there. When you're ready — even partly ready — you can try a different question. One that has somewhere to go.

Grab a pen. Write "Why me?" at the top of a page. Give it five minutes — write everything that question wants to say.

Then draw a line underneath it. Below the line, write: "What now?" Give yourself five more minutes to answer that instead.

You don't need to solve anything. Just notice what's different about the second question.

The Difference Between Pain and Purpose

Let's be careful with the word "purpose."

People sometimes weaponise it.

They say things like, "Everything happens for a reason," or "You'll see why this was meant to happen," and it can feel like someone is trying to tidy up your pain with a slogan.

That's not what I mean.

Purpose is not a reason.

Purpose is a direction.

Purpose doesn't mean you are gladthis happened.

Purpose means: Given that this happened, you're going to live on purpose anyway.

That's the turning point.

And it's often quiet.

It's not fireworks.

It's not a dramatic speech.

It's a decision you make when you're tired of waiting.

What Happens If You Don't Shift the Question

If you stay in "Why me?" too long, here's what can happen:

- you stay emotionally tied to the event
- you keep negotiating with the past
- you keep feeling powerless
- you keep waiting for closure
- you delay rebuilding
- you live in a loop instead of a life

Again—no judgement.

Just honesty.

That question is expensive.

What Becomes Possible When You Shift to "What Now?"

When you shift to "What now?", you reclaim something trauma tried to steal: agency.

You start noticing small choices again.

You start making decisions based on what helps, not what hurts.

You start building evidence that you can carry this season.

And this is where post-traumatic growth becomes practical.

Not because you forced meaning.

Because you started moving with intention.

You started making choices that slowly reshape your identity, your relationships, your values, and your future.

That's how people change for the better.

Not in one moment.

In a sequence of small, steady choices.

Say This to Yourself

If you're caught in the "why" loop, borrow this:

"I may never get a satisfying 'why.' But I can choose a powerful 'what now.'"

Or simpler:

"No closure doesn't mean no future."

The Turning Point Is a Question You Choose

You're allowed to ask "Why me?"

You're allowed to grieve.

You're allowed to be angry.

But you're also allowed to stop paying rent to a question that can't give you your life back.

The turning point isn't an answer.

It's a shift.

From "Why me?"

To "What now?"

And the moment you ask "What now?"—even quietly—you've already started rebuilding.

Part Two: Rebuilding on Purpose

Part Two is where the rebuild begins in earnest. You'll find tools, practices, and frameworks — but more than that, you'll find a sequence. Each chapter builds on the one before it. You don't need to feel ready. You just need to be willing to take the next honest step.

"Well done is better than well said."

— **Benjamin Franklin,** *Poor Richard* **(1737)**

9

You Don't Need More Advice — You Need Tools That Work

Before growth becomes possible, stability must exist. This chapter addresses the first domain of recovery that research reliably validates: personal strength — specifically, the ability to function under sustained pressure. What follows is not a wellness programme. It's a floor.

If you've been waiting until you feel ready to do the bigger work, this chapter is where you get ready. Not by thinking harder about it. But by building a floor.

This chapter is not a wellness programme. It is not a self-care checklist. It is a floor — the minimum viable set of behaviours that keeps you functional on the hard days. Not thriving. Just functional. That is enough to start.

That's not a philosophy. That's neuroscience. A nervous system that is running on empty — under-slept, under-nourished, under-supported, and over-stimulated — does not have the spare capacity to process, integrate, or rebuild. It is in survival mode. And survival mode is not a growth environment.

Before growth becomes possible, stability must exist.

After trauma, people will hand you advice like they're throwing life jackets from the shore.

Some of it is well-meaning.

Some of it is unhelpful.

Some of it is just noise.

And if you've tried a bunch of things already, you might be at the point where you're thinking:

"Okay… but what actually helps?"

Not in theory.

In real life.

On a Tuesday.

When you're tired.

When you're triggered.

When you're trying to rebuild without turning your life into a full-time self-improvement project.

That's what this chapter is for.

You're Overwhelmed, So You Either Do Everything or Nothing

Here's the problem with "tools" after trauma:

People either go into full control mode—trying to fix everything at once…or they shut down completely, because it all feels like too much.

So the days become inconsistent.

One day you're motivated and doing all the right things.

The next day you can't get off the couch and you feel like you've failed.

That doesn't mean you're lazy.

That means you're overwhelmed.

And overwhelmed people don't need more tasks.

They need a simpler system.

Lie #9: "If I Do All the Right Things, I'll Feel Better Fast"

This lie sounds productive, but it's a setup:

"If I do all the right things, I'll feel better fast."

Sometimes you will feel better quickly.

But rebuilding is not a straight line.

And if you expect instant results, you'll quit the tools that actually work—because the tools that work are often boring.

They're repetitive.

They're unglamorous.

And they're powerful over time.

Tools Don't Fix You – Tools Stabilise You

Here's the reframe that makes tools usable:

Tools don't fix you.

Tools stabilise you.

Stability is what gives you access to better choices.

Better choices are what create momentum.

Momentum is what makes growth possible.

So you're not doing self-care to be trendy.

You're building a stable base so your nervous system can stop acting like every day is an emergency.

Your System Needs Safety Signals

After trauma, your mind and body start looking for safety cues.

If your mind and body can't find them, they stay on alert.

That's why small stabilising behaviours matter so much. They're safety signals.

Sleep is a safety signal.

Food is a safety signal.

Movement is a safety signal.

Connection is a safety signal.

Boundaries are a safety signal.

Structure is a safety signal.

So the goal isn't to become a perfect person.

The goal is to send your system enough safety signals that it can come out of survival mode more often.

The Enemy: The "All-or-Nothing" Trap

This is the enemy that ruins tools: "All-or-nothing."

It sounds like:

- "If I can't do it properly, I won't do it at all."
- "If I miss a day, I've failed."
- "If I can't do the full routine, it's pointless."

But rebuilding doesn't respond to perfection.

Rebuilding responds to consistency.

Small, consistent steps beat big, occasional efforts.

That's how your system learns.

Choose a Minimum Set That You Can Actually Maintain

Here's the plan for this chapter:

Step 1: Pick tools that calm your system, not tools that impress you

Because this is about function, not identity.

Step 2: Create a minimum version for hard days

So you don't quit when life is heavy.

Step 3: Stack your tools around daily anchors

So they become automatic.

Step 4: Track proof, not perfection

Because proof builds hope.

That's how you build a toolkit you'll actually use.

Tool 1: Sleep – The Foundation Most People Underestimate

If your sleep is off, everything feels harder.

Your emotions feel bigger.

Your thoughts feel darker.

Your patience gets thinner.

Your coping gets weaker.

Sleep doesn't solve your life, but it makes your life solvable.

Minimum version for hard days:

- pick a consistent "lights out" time (even if sleep isn't perfect)
- reduce the late-night scrolling by just 10 minutes
- create one small cue that says "we're winding down" (tea, shower, book, music)

You're not chasing perfect sleep.

You're building a signal of safety.

Tool 2: Movement – Not Fitness, Regulation

When people hear the word "exercise," they often think of punishment.

This isn't punishment.

This is regulation.

Movement helps your nervous system discharge some of the stress chemicals it's been carrying. Movement helps your body remember it can move through discomfort.

Minimum version:

- a 10-minute walk
- stretching for five minutes
- one song and move your body to it
- step outside and breathe for two minutes

The point isn't performance.

The point is telling your system: "We're alive, and we're moving."

Tool 3: Food and Hydration – The Most Basic Stabiliser

When your body is underfed or dehydrated, your mind becomes more dramatic.

That's not a character flaw.

That's biology.

Minimum version:

- drink a glass of water before coffee
- add one stable meal a day that you can repeat
- don't let the day run on pure adrenaline

This isn't a diet chapter.

This is a stability chapter.

Tool 4: Structure – A Simple Day Plan That Prevents Spirals

A lot of people resist structure because it feels boring.

But after trauma, structure is kindness.

Because structure reduces decision fatigue.

And fewer decisions means fewer opportunities to spiral.

Minimum version:

- choose three things for today: one necessary task, one self-supporting task, one connecting task
- write them down
- do them in any order
- call it a win

That's enough.

Tool 5: Boundaries – The Tool That Protects Everything Else

Trauma can make you feel like you have to keep everyone happy to stay safe.

But rebuilding requires boundaries.

Because without boundaries, your energy leaks everywhere.

Minimum version:

- one honest "no" this week
- one pause before you say yes
- one sentence you practise so you don't over-explain

Try this boundary sentence:

"I can't do that right now, but thank you for thinking of me."

Simple. Clean. No courtroom.

Tool 6: Connection – One Safe Person Beats a Hundred Likes

You don't need a crowd.

You need safety.

Minimum version:

- message one person and tell them one honest sentence
- sit with someone without performing *fine*
- ask for a 10-minute check-in

Connection isn't a luxury.

It's regulation.

Tool 7: Writing – Getting It Out of Your Head and Onto Paper

You don't need to be a writer.

You just need somewhere for the pressure to go.

Minimum version:

- write three sentences:
    1. "Today feels…"
    2. "What I need is…"
    3. "The next step is…"

That's it.

You're not writing a memoir.

You're creating clarity.

Tool 8: Meaning-Making – Only When You're Ready

This is important: meaning-making is powerful, but it can't be forced.

If you try to force meaning too early, meaning-making can feel like spiritual bypassing—like you're trying to tidy up pain with a neat story.

So we do meaning-making gently.

Minimum version:

- "What has this taught me about what matters?"
- "What do I want to carry forward?"
- "What do I refuse to become because of this?"

Meaning is not a reason.

Meaning is a direction.

Try This Today: Build Your "Minimum Toolkit" (10 Minutes)

Grab a pen and write:

"On hard days, my minimum toolkit is…"

Pick only 5. Not 15. Five.

1. Sleep minimum: ____________________
2. Movement minimum: ________________
3. Food/water minimum: ________________
4. Connection minimum: ________________
5. One stabilising task minimum: ___________

Now write this sentence underneath:

"If I do my minimum toolkit, the day counts."

Because it does.

You're not aiming for a perfect day.

You're aiming for a stable day.

What Happens If You Don't Have Tools

If you don't have tools, you default to whatever coping mechanism is easiest in the moment.

Sometimes that coping is fine.

Sometimes it costs you later—through sleep, mood, health, relationships, or shame.

Tools don't make you superior.

Tools make you steadier.

What Becomes Possible When You Use Your Toolkit Consistently

When you use your toolkit consistently, you start noticing changes that actually matter:

- fewer spirals
- faster recovery after hard moments
- clearer thinking
- more stable moods
- better decisions
- more confidence in yourself

And this is where post-traumatic growth becomes more than a concept.

Because growth isn't only insight.

Growth is behaviour that becomes identity.

Say This to Yourself

If you're tempted to quit because you can't do it perfectly, borrow this:

"Minimum is still movement."

Or:

"Stability first. Growth follows."

Your Toolkit Is How You Take Yourself Seriously

This chapter isn't here to make you better.

It's here to make you steadier.

Because steadiness is what makes the next step possible.

So start small.

Pick a minimum toolkit.

Use it on hard days.

And let that be your proof that you're rebuilding.

One stable day at a time.

A Bridge to What Comes Next

Once this floor is in place — even imperfectly — Chapter 14 builds on top of it with practices designed for growth rather than just stability. The distinction matters. This chapter keeps you standing. That one starts moving you forward.

"When you come out of the storm, you won't be the same person who walked in. That's what this storm's all about."

— Haruki Murakami, Kafka on the Shore (2002)

10

The First Time You Notice You're Not the Same

There's a moment that comes for a lot of people—sometimes months after the hard thing, sometimes years—where you catch yourself doing something you didn't expect.

You say no… and you don't apologise for it.

You reach out to someone… and you actually mean it.

You feel a wave of gratitude for something small and ordinary, and this gratitude hits deeper than it used to.

You laugh—properly laugh—for the first time in ages, and it surprises you.

And for a second you think, "Wait… am I changing?"

Not back to who you were.

But into someone else.

Someone a little sturdier.

Someone a little clearer.

Someone who's been shaped by what happened—but not swallowed by it.

You Think "Better" Means Pretending It Didn't Hurt

Here's the problem with the phrase "change for the better."

A lot of people hear that and assume it means you're supposed to spin pain into a positive story.

Like the only acceptable outcome is: "I'm grateful it happened."

No.

That's not what we're doing here.

Because "better" doesn't mean you approve of what happened.

"Better" means: you're rebuilding in a way that creates real strength, real clarity, and a life that fits again.

Lie # 9: "If I'm Still Hurting, I Can't Be Growing"

This lie keeps people stuck in an either/or mindset:

"If I'm still hurting, I can't be growing."

But growth and pain can coexist.

In fact, in this context, they often do.

You can still grieve and still become wiser.

You can still have hard days and still make better choices.

You can still feel the weight of what happened and still build a future.

Growth Isn't a Mood – It's a Pattern

This is where the research is quietly reassuring.

When researchers Richard Tedeschi and Lawrence Calhoun began studying what happens to people after trauma, they noticed something: many people weren't only describing distress.

They were also describing *change*.

Not the glossy, motivational kind.

The grounded, lived kind.

Patterns.

And over time, those patterns have been refined and expanded by many researchers and clinicians in this space.

So instead of treating growth like a magical personality trait—something you either have or don't have—we can treat it like something more practical:

Growth shows up in specific areas, and those areas are learnable.

The Five Areas People Often Change

If you're wondering, "What does growth even look like?"—this is the clearest answer I can give you.

People tend to describe positive change in five broad areas.

Not all five. Not all at once. Not in a straight line.

But these are the common places it shows up.

1) Relationships: You Get Clearer About Who Matters

After trauma, a lot of people stop tolerating surface-level connections.

They become more selective.

They care less about keeping everyone happy.

They feel more drawn to honesty, depth, and real support.

Sometimes relationships strengthen.

Sometimes some relationships fall away.

Either way, there's often a new clarity:

Connection matters. And you are going to be more intentional about it.

2) Personal Strength: You Realise You Can Carry Hard Things

This one is easy to misunderstand.

It doesn't mean you feel strong all the time.

It means you can look back and say:

You didn't think you could get through that… but you did.

Strength here isn't bravado.

It's evidence.

It's the quiet confidence that comes from surviving a chapter you didn't choose—and rebuilding anyway.

3) New Possibilities: Your Life Opens in a Different Direction

Sometimes trauma shuts doors.

But it can also change your priorities so much that you start noticing doors you never would have walked through before.

New work. New friendships. New interests. New boundaries. New ways of living.

Not because you're over what happened to you.

But because you're no longer living by the old blueprint.

And when the blueprint changes, possibilities change.

4) Appreciation: Ordinary Life Starts Feeling Less Ordinary

This isn't forced gratitude.

This is the kind that sneaks up on you.

A quiet morning.

A simple meal.

A safe conversation.

A moment of calm.

After trauma, those moments can hit differently—not because life is perfect, but because you know how quickly life can change.

So you notice what you used to rush past.

5) Meaning and Spiritual Change: You Start Asking Deeper Questions

This isn't about religion, and it also isn't *not* about religion.

It's bigger than that.

A lot of people find themselves asking:

"What actually matters now?"

"What kind of person do I want to be?"

"What do I believe about life?"

"What do I want my story to stand for?"

Sometimes these events deepen faith.

Sometimes they reshape them.

Sometimes they create meaning in a more personal, human way.

But the common thread is this: your values become clearer.

The Enemy: Thinking You Have to Achieve Growth

Now, a warning—because this is where people accidentally turn growth into another performance.

They start treating these five areas like a checklist.

"Do I have that one yet?"

"What about that one?"

"Why am I not growing faster?"

That's not the point.

The point is to notice what's already shifting, and then support it with the next step.

Growth isn't something you force.

Growth is something you *build conditions for.*

Spot the Pattern, Then Support It

Here's the plan for this chapter:

Step 1: Notice where change is already happening

Even if it's small.

Step 2: Choose one area to strengthen

Not all five.

Step 3: Take one action that supports that area

Because growth becomes real when it shows up in behaviour.

Try This Today: The "Five Areas" Check-In (10 Minutes)

Grab a pen and write:

"If I'm changing for the better, I'm noticing it most in..."

Now answer these, quickly, without overthinking:

1. **Relationships:** One shift I've noticed is...

___

2. **Strength:** One thing I can handle now that I couldn't before is...

___

3. **Possibilities:** One new direction I'm more open to is...

___

4. **Appreciation:** One ordinary thing that feels more meaningful now is...

___

5. **Meaning:** One value that feels clearer now is...

___

Now circle **one** answer and finish this sentence:

"The next step I can take to support this is..."

___

Smallest version. Within 24 hours.

That's how you turn a hopeful idea into a lived reality.

Say This to Yourself

If you need a line to borrow after this chapter, use this:

"I don't have to be okay to be growing."

Growth Has a Shape

If you've been wondering whether you're changing, this is how you'll know.

Growth has a shape.

It shows up in relationships, strength, possibilities, appreciation, and meaning.

Not as a perfect transformation.

As a real rebuild.

And now that you can see the shape, you can start supporting it—one small step at a time.

"We do not grow absolutely, chronologically. We grow sometimes in one dimension, and not in another; unevenly."

— Anaïs Nin, The Diary of Anaïs Nin

11

The Weird Part About Getting Better

Research consistently shows that people who survive serious disruption don't just recover their sense of self — they rebuild it with more precision. This chapter is about that process: not finding yourself, but constructing yourself.

One of the strangest parts of rebuilding is this:

Sometimes getting better feels worse.

You take a step forward… and suddenly you feel more emotional.

You start being honest… and you feel more exposed.

You reconnect with life… and you feel more anxious.

You stop numbing… and everything you avoided shows up at once.

And that can make you think:

"I knew it. I'm going backwards."

But you're not.

You're just meeting reality again.

You Think Discomfort Means You're Failing

Here's the problem with discomfort in the growth stage:

People interpret it as a sign something is wrong.

They think:

- "This shouldn't feel this hard."
- "If I were healing properly, I'd feel calmer."
- "If I was growing, I'd feel more positive."
- "If I was doing this right, I wouldn't be this triggered."

And because discomfort feels like danger, they pull back.

They stop doing the things that were actually helping.

They retreat into avoidance, distraction, or old coping mechanisms.

Not because they're lazy.

Because discomfort can feel like a threat.

Lie #11: "If It's Right, It Should Feel Easy"

This is one of the most seductive lies:

"If it's right, it should feel easy."

But that's not how change works.

Most real growth feels awkward at first.

Most real rebuilding feels clunky.

Most real confidence is built through uncomfortable repetition.

And after trauma, discomfort can feel even louder because your nervous system is already on alert.

So you're not just facing discomfort.

You're facing discomfort with a system that's scanning for danger.

That's a different game.

Discomfort Is Often a Sign You're Rebuilding, Not Breaking

Here's the reframe that saves people from quitting too early:

Discomfort is often a sign you're rebuilding, not breaking.

Think about it.

If you've been living in survival mode—numbing, avoiding, bracing, performing "fine"—then stepping into honesty, connection, boundaries, or new routines will feel unfamiliar.

And unfamiliar can feel unsafe.

Not because it *is* unsafe, but because your system doesn't recognise this unfamiliarity yet.

So the goal isn't to eliminate discomfort.

The goal is to learn the difference between:

- discomfort that is growth

and

- discomfort that is harm

That distinction is everything.

Your Nervous System Is Updating Its Settings

If trauma was an earthquake, then rebuilding requires construction.

And construction is noisy.

Dusty.

Disruptive.

It involves temporary mess.

So of course it doesn't feel like peace straight away.

Your nervous system is updating its settings.

It's learning:

"This is safe now."

"This is possible now."

"I can handle this now."

"I don't have to brace all day."

But that learning happens through experience.

Not through logic.

You don't convince your body with a lecture.

You convince it with repetition.

Safe repetition over time.

The Enemy: Quitting in the Uncomfortable Middle

This is where a lot of people get derailed.

They begin rebuilding. They see progress. Then discomfort spikes and they think something is wrong.

They quit in the uncomfortable middle.

And the uncomfortable middle is exactly where growth happens.

It's the stage where you're no longer who you were…

…but you don't feel like the new version of you yet either.

So it feels unstable.

That's normal.

It's also temporary—if you keep going.

Normalise the Mess and Keep It Safe

Here's the plan for this stage:

Step 1: Name the discomfort

So it stops feeling like a mystery threat.

Step 2: Identify what kind of discomfort it is

Growth discomfort or harm discomfort.

Step 3: Choose a steady action

Not a dramatic one. A steady one.

Step 4: Repeat

Because repetition builds safety.

That's how you move through the uncomfortable middle without quitting.

To make it even clearer, here are two simple categories.

Growth Discomfort

This often sounds like:

- "I feel nervous, but I know this matters."
- "This feels unfamiliar, but it's good for me."
- "I'm scared, but I'm proud I'm trying."
- "I feel exposed, but I'm being real."

Growth discomfort usually comes with *meaning*.

It's uncomfortable, but it points somewhere.

Harm Discomfort

This often sounds like:

- "I feel unsafe."
- "I feel like I'm betraying myself."
- "This crosses my boundaries."
- "I feel worse every time, not stronger over time."

Harm discomfort is a warning.

It's your system saying, "This is not okay."

This book isn't telling you to push through harm.

This book is helping you stay with growth discomfort long enough for it to become strength.

Try This Today: The Discomfort Decoder (10 Minutes)

Grab a pen and answer these questions:

1. What feels uncomfortable right now?

Be specific.

---

2. What did this discomfort show up right after?

A boundary? A conversation? A new habit? A decision?

---

3. Is this discomfort telling me "this is new," or "this is dangerous"?

If it's new, it often comes with nerves and uncertainty but still feels aligned.

If it's dangerous, it often comes with dread, self-betrayal, or a sense of being harmed.

---

4. What would the smallest steady action be that supports me today?

Not a leap. A step.

Now do the smallest steady action.

Then give yourself credit for staying in the middle instead of quitting.

Say This to Yourself

If you're in the uncomfortable middle, borrow this:

"This feels uncomfortable because it's new — not because it's wrong."

Or, if you need something shorter:

"The middle is messy. Keep going."

Discomfort Isn't the Enemy – Quitting Is

You don't have to love the discomfort.

You don't have to rush it away.

You just need to learn what it means.

Some discomfort is growth.

Some discomfort is harm.

Your job isn't to be fearless.

Your job is to be steady.

Because the uncomfortable middle is where your future is built.

"No man is an island, entire of itself."

— **John Donne,** *Devotions upon Emergent Occasions* **(1624)**

12

The Moment You Realise You're Carrying It Alone

One of the most documented effects of major trauma is that it reorganises your relationships — stripping some away, deepening others, and occasionally introducing new ones. That's the domain Post-Traumatic Growth researchers call Relating to Others, and it's worth examining honestly.

A lot of people don't realise they're isolated until they have one of those moments.

You're in the car, driving somewhere normal, and suddenly you feel it:

You're doing this by yourself."

Or you're in a room full of people and you feel completely alone.

Or you catch yourself editing the truth again—saying you're fine when you're not—because you don't want to make things awkward.

And it hits you:

You don't actually have a place to put this.

That moment matters.

Because trauma is heavy.

And heavy things are not meant to be carried alone.

Isolation Makes Everything Harder

Here's the problem with isolation:

It doesn't just make you lonely.

It makes your symptoms louder.

When you're isolated, your mind has no interruption from its own loops.

Your nervous system has fewer cues of safety.

Your pain becomes the only voice in the room.

You start believing thoughts that would sound ridiculous if you said them out loud to someone safe.

Isolation doesn't always look like having no people.

Sometimes isolation looks like having people around you–but no one who really knows what's going on.

And that kind of loneliness can be even sharper.

Lie # 11: "I Don't Want to Burden Anyone"

This lie is incredibly common, especially in people who are competent, responsible, and used to being the strong one.

"I don't want to burden anyone."

So you keep it to yourself.

You tell yourself they have enough going on.

You tell yourself you should be able to handle it.

You tell yourself you'll talk when you're better.

But here's the issue:

Waiting until you're better is often how you stay stuck.

Because support isn't the reward for healing.

Support is one of the ingredients.

Support Isn't Weakness – It's How Humans Regulate

Let's reframe this properly.

Support isn't weakness.

Support is a nervous system tool.

Humans calm down in a safe connection.

That's not a motivational quote. That's biology.

A regulated nervous system is easier to live in.

A regulated nervous system thinks more clearly.

A regulated nervous system makes better decisions.

A regulated nervous system rebuilds faster.

So when you seek support, you're not being dramatic.

You're being smart.

You Don't Need Everyone – You Need Safety

This is where people get stuck, because they aim for the wrong target.

They think support means:

- telling everyone everything
- having long emotional conversations
- being vulnerable with the wrong people
- turning your trauma into a public story

No wonder they avoid seeking support.

But that's not what support needs to look like.

Support isn't about everyone.

Support is about *safety*.

One safe person can change your trajectory.

One conversation that is honest can reduce shame.

One moment of being understood can quiet your nervous system.

So the goal isn't a big audience.

The goal is a safe container.

The Enemy: Unsupportive People (Even When They Mean Well)

This part matters because sometimes the issue isn't you.

Sometimes the people around you simply don't have the skills.

They might be good people, but they respond with:

- quick fixes
- forced positivity
- minimising
- comparison
- advice that skips reality
- changing the subject
- making it about them
- getting uncomfortable and shutting down

That doesn't mean you're unlovable.

It means they're not the right container.

And you need to know the difference.

Because trying to get emotional safety from someone who can't offer it will make you feel worse.

So we're going to be selective.

Not bitter.

Selective.

Build a Support System Without Making It a Drama

Here's the plan for this chapter:

Step 1: Identify who is safe

Not who *should* be safe. Who actually is.

Step 2: Start small

One honest sentence. Not your whole life story.

Step 3: Ask for a specific kind of support

Not just the words "help me." Ask for something concrete.

Step 4: Expand slowly

Support is built. It's not magically found.

That's how you stop carrying your trauma alone without overwhelming yourself.

Try This Today: The "Safe Person" Filter (10 Minutes)

Grab a pen and write the names of 3–5 people in your world.

Now, next to each name, answer these questions with a simple yes or no:

1. **Do I feel calmer after talking to them?**
2. **Do they listen without rushing to fix me?**
3. **Do they handle emotion without getting weird?**
4. **Do they respect my boundaries?**
5. **Do they keep my confidence safe?**

If someone scores mostly "no," they're not a safe container for this part of your life.

They might still be a friend, a colleague, or a family member,but they're not your support person for this.

If someone scores mostly "yes," that's your starting point.

Now choose one person and send a message that is small and clear.

Here are a few you can copy:

- "Hey, I've been having a harder time than I've been letting on. Can I talk for 10 minutes this week?"
- "I'm not okay yet. I don't need solutions—just someone to listen."
- "I'm working through something and I'd value your steady presence. Are you free for a quick chat?"

Short. Simple. Honest.

No performance required.

What Support Actually Looks Like (In Real Life)

Support isn't always a deep conversation.

Sometimes support is:

- a walk with someone who doesn't interrogate you
- a meal where you feel safe enough to breathe

- a therapist or coach who gives you structure
- a support group where you don't have to explain yourself
- a friend who can handle the truth without trying to tidy it up
- someone who checks in consistently, not once and then disappears

Support is consistency plus safety.

That's the formula.

What to Do If You Don't Have Safe People Yet

This is important, because some readers will think:

"I don't have anyone."

If that's you, it doesn't mean you're doomed.

It means your next step is to *build* support.

And sometimes that starts with:

- one professional support relationship
- one community space
- one group
- one online forum that is well moderated
- one person you reach out to whom you've underestimated
- one step toward not doing this work alone

Support can be built.

You don't need to wait until you magically find your people.

You start with one safe connection and expand.

Say This to Yourself

If the "burden" thought shows up, borrow this:

"Asking for support isn't weakness. It's how humans have always survived hard things."

Or:

"I don't need everyone. I need to be safe."

You Were Never Meant to Carry This Alone

You don't have to turn your pain into a public story.

You don't have to overshare.

You don't have to find the perfect words.

You just need one safe place to put the truth.

Because when the truth is held safely, your nervous system settles.

And when your nervous system settles, you can rebuild.

One step at a time.

"Try again. Fail again. Fail better."

— Samuel Beckett, Worstward Ho (1983)

13

The Day You Think, "I'm Back at the Start"

Setbacks are not evidence that growth isn't happening. In Post-Traumatic Growth research, the experience of being knocked back and continuing anyway is precisely what consolidates personal strength — not the falling, but the returning.

David's Story

David had been doing well. Eight steady weeks — better sleep, back at work part-time, a few good evenings with his kids. He'd started to feel something he was cautious about naming: normal.

Then his brother visited for the weekend. Nothing went wrong. The visit was fine. But on the Monday morning after his brother left, David woke up and couldn't get out of bed until noon. He felt hollowed out. He cried in the shower and didn't know why.

His first thought was: I've lost everything I built.

He hadn't. What had happened was that his nervous system had spent eight weeks functioning at a high level, and the relaxation of a familiar, safe visit had let the accumulated weight surface. The emotion had been waiting. Safety had finally allowed it through. The setback wasn't a regression. It was evidence that he'd built enough stability to finally feel what he'd been carrying.

Here's what that can look like in practice.

There's a day that catches almost everyone.

You've had a few steady weeks. You've been doing your minimum toolkit. You've taken a few next steps. You've started to feel more like yourself.

And then… something happens.

A bad sleep.

A comment.

A memory.

A date on the calendar.

A smell, a song, a place.

A random wave of emotion that hits like it came out of nowhere.

And you think:

"Great. I'm back at the start."

That thought can flatten you.

Not because the hard moment is unbearable, but because you interpret it as failure.

So let's fix that interpretation.

You Mistake a Setback for Proof You're Not Healing

Setbacks feel like betrayal.

You thought you were past this. You thought you were doing better. You thought you were finally getting somewhere.

And then your nervous system says, "Nope."

So you start asking:

- "What's wrong with me?"
- "Why am I still like this?"
- "Am I ever going to be okay?"
- "Was all that progress fake?"

That's the problem.

Not the setback itself.

The meaning you attach to it.

Because if you tell yourself setbacks mean you're failing, you'll start quitting things that were helping.

And quitting turns a setback into a slide.

Lie #13: "If I Was Really Healing, I Wouldn't Feel Like This Again"

This is the lie that turns one hard day into a hard week:

"If I was really healing, I wouldn't feel like this again."

But healing isn't a straight line.

Rebuilding isn't linear.

Growth isn't a neat staircase.

It's more like:

two steps forward, one step back… and then forward again.

Sometimes you don't even go back.

Sometimes you hit a deeper layer.

And deeper layers can feel like regression even when you're actually processing something more honestly.

A Setback Is Information, Not a Verdict

Here's the reframe that saves people from spiralling:

A setback is information, not a verdict.

It's your system saying:

"Something here still needs attention."

"Something here still feels unsafe."

"Something here is asking to be integrated."

That's not proof you're broken.

That's proof you're human.

And—this matters—a setback can actually be a sign of growth if you respond to it differently than you used to.

Because growth isn't about never getting triggered.

Growth is about what you do next.

Triggers, Fatigue, and the Rebuild Cycle

Setbacks often happen for simple reasons that people overlook.

1) Triggers

Your brain connected a cue to danger. That cue can be obvious or subtle. When it shows up, your system reacts before you can think.

2) Fatigue

When you're tired, your coping resources drop. Everything feels bigger. Your window of tolerance shrinks.

3) Accumulated stress

Sometimes nothing dramatic happened today. You just had ten small stressors. Your system hit its limit.

4) Milestones and anniversaries

Dates, seasons, places, and reminders can bring waves you didn't plan for.

5) Progress itself

Sometimes you've been steady, but the moment your system relaxes, emotions that were held back show up.

So yes—setbacks can be intense.

But they're not random.

They're signals.

And signals can be worked with.

The Enemy: The "Screw It" Spiral

The "screw it" spiral.

It goes like this:

Setback → shame → self-attack → withdrawal → coping slips → more shame → more setback

And once you're in that spiral, it's easy to think:

"What's the point?"

The point is that you don't need to prevent every setback.

You just need a way to stop the spiral early.

What a Hard Day Actually Needs

There is no plan for a hard day. Plans are for when you have capacity. When you don't, plans become another thing you're failing at.

What a hard day actually requires is one thing: don't let it become the story. Don't let the wave convince you it's the whole ocean. Name it for what it is — a setback, a wave, a harder-than-usual day — and then do one stabilising thing. Not five. One.

That's the entire instruction for today.

Try This: Two Sentences (No Timer)

Write one sentence: "This is a setback, not a verdict." Then write one sentence starting with: "The one thing I can do in the next hour is..." That's it. That's enough.

The Most Important Skill: Clean Repair

Setbacks are not the problem.

Shame is the problem.

So the most important skill you can build is repair.

Here's clean repair:

- "Okay. That was a hard moment."
- "It makes sense that I'm feeling this."
- "What do I need right now?"
- "What's the smallest step I can take?"
- "I'm still on my side."

That last line is the difference between relapse and recovery.

Not in a dramatic sense.

In a daily-life sense.

If you abandon yourself after a setback, you teach your system you're not safe with you.

If you stay with yourself after a setback, you teach your system the opposite.

That's how self-trust grows.

How to Tell If You're Actually Growing

Here's a question that cuts through the panic:

"Do I recover faster than I used to?"

Growth doesn't mean you never fall apart.

Growth means you come back quicker.

Growth means you don't stay lost as long.

Growth means you have tools now.

Growth means you can name the wave, stabilise, and take a step.

That is real progress.

Even if it doesn't feel inspiring.

What Becomes Possible When You Treat Setbacks as Part of the Process

When you treat setbacks as part of the process, you build resilience without trying.

You build a kind of confidence that isn't based on perfect days.

You build steadiness.

You learn that you can have a hard day and still stay in motion.

That's a superpower.

Not because you become unshakeable.

Because you become repairable.

Say This to Yourself

If you hit a setback and feel the panic rising, borrow this:

"This is a wave, not a verdict."

Or:

"A hard day doesn't erase my progress."

You're Not Back at the Start – You're In the Middle

If you're having a setback, you're not failing.

You're in the middle.

And the middle is messy.

So don't ask, "Why am I like this?"

Ask:

"What does my system need right now?"

Then do the smallest stabilising thing.

Take one next step.

And remind yourself:

You're not back at the start.

You're rebuilding.

"We are what we repeatedly do. Excellence, then, is not an act, but a habit."

— **Will Durant,** *The Story of Philosophy* **(1926)**

14

Most People Are Waiting for a Breakthrough That Never Comes

Chapter 9 gave you a floor. Chapter 13 told you what to do when you have a setback. This chapter gives you a foundation.

Those are different things. A floor is what you build so you don't fall through. A foundation is what you build so something can stand on top of it. They look similar from the outside. The difference is in the intention.

If you've been doing the minimum toolkit from Chapter 9 — even imperfectly, even intermittently — you have a floor. You're stable enough to start asking a different kind of question. Not "how do I get through today?" but "what am I actually building toward?"

The practices in this chapter are not for crisis days. They're for the days between crises — the ordinary, incremental days where growth actually happens. They require slightly more of you than the floor does. And they give significantly more back.

When the basic scaffolding of stability is in place, something shifts. Post-Traumatic Growth researchers call it New Possibilities — the recognition that the life ahead doesn't have to replicate the life before. This chapter is about building deliberately toward that.

A lot of people secretly believe growth happens like this:

One day you wake up and you're different.

You have a breakthrough. You feel clear. You feel strong. You feel certain. You finally get it.

And then life becomes easier.

That story is comforting.

It's also mostly wrong.

Not because breakthroughs never happen.

But because most real change doesn't arrive like lightning.

It arrives like repetition.

Quiet. Unsexy. Consistent.

And if you're waiting for a breakthrough before you start living again, you'll stay stuck in the waiting room.

You Keep Looking for the Big Moment Instead of Building the Pattern

Here's the problem with breakthrough-thinking:

It makes you judge your progress based on how you *feel.*

So if you have a good day, you think, "I'm healing."

If you have a hard day, you think, "I'm back at the start."

And that emotional rollercoaster is exhausting.

It also makes you miss the real signal of growth: patterns.

Growth is not a mood.

Growth is a pattern that shows up in what you do—especially when it's hard.

Lie #14: "Once I Feel Better, I'll Do Better"

This lie sounds logical:

"Once I feel better, I'll do better."

But most of the time, it works the other way around:

You do better—small, steady actions—and then you start feeling better more often.

That doesn't mean you force yourself.

It means you stop waiting for your emotions to give you permission to rebuild.

Because emotions are weather.

They change.

Practices are structure.

They hold you steady when the weather shifts.

Growth Happens Through Practices That Create Evidence

Here's the reframe:

Growth doesn't happen because you understand something once.

Growth happens because you practise something until your system believes it.

Your brain changes through evidence.

Your nervous system settles through repetition.

Your identity shifts through behaviour that you repeat long enough to call it "me."

So we're not hunting breakthroughs.

We're building practices.

Your System Learns Through Repetition

After trauma, your system becomes cautious.

It is not impressed by your intentions.

Your system wants proof.

You can tell yourself you're safe now a thousand times.

But if your body doesn't *experience* safety through steady routines, boundaries, connection, and action, it won't update.

So when people say, "Time heals," that's only partly true.

Time helps… when it's filled with the right practices.

If time is filled with avoidance, isolation, and self-attack, time doesn't heal.

Time just passes.

Practice is what changes things.

The Enemy: The All-at-Once Fix

Another growth killer is the all-at-once fix.

You get inspired and decide:

- "I'm changing everything starting Monday."
- "New routine. New diet. New mindset. New life."

And then life happens.

You miss a day.

You feel disappointed.

You conclude you can't stick to anything.

And you give up.

That cycle doesn't mean you lack discipline.

It means the plan was too big for your nervous system.

After trauma, the system prefers *small and safe.*

So we build growth in a way your system can actually accept.

Choose a Practice, Make It Minimum, Repeat It

Here's the plan for this chapter:

Step 1: Choose one practice that supports stability

Not ten.

Step 2: Create a minimum version

So you can do it even on hard days.

Step 3: Attach it to a daily anchor

So it becomes automatic.

Step 4: Track proof

Because proof builds hope, and hope builds momentum.

That's how growth becomes real.

Not because you had a breakthrough.

Because you built a practice.

The Five Practices That Create the Most Growth

I'm going to keep this simple and practical. These are not the only practices—but they're the ones that tend to have the biggest impact.

Practice 1: The Next Step Practice

Every day, one question:

What is the next step that makes your life 5% more stable?

Then do the smallest version.

This practice kills confusion. It builds momentum.

Practice 2: The Regulation Practice

One thing a day that calms your system:

- movement
- breath
- nature
- music
- a shower
- stretching
- a short walk
- silence

The point isn't relaxation.

The point is nervous system safety.

Practice 3: The Truth Practice

One honest sentence a day.

Not a diary entry. One sentence.

"Today I feel…"

or

"What I need is…"

or

"The truth is…"

Truth stops you from performing.

And performance is where people get stuck.

Practice 4: The Boundary Practice

One small self-respecting action a week.

A pause. A no. A limit. A clean sentence.

Boundaries rebuild self-trust.

Self-trust rebuilds your life.

Practice 5: The Connection Practice

One safe connection a week.

A message. A coffee. A call. A session. A group.

Connection regulates your nervous system and reduces shame.

These practices are not dramatic.

But they are powerful.

Because they create evidence.

Try This Today: Build Your "Growth Practice" (10 Minutes)

Grab a pen and write:

"If I choose one practice for the next 14 days, it will be…"

Pick one:

- next step

- regulation
- truth
- boundary
- connection

Now write the minimum version:

"The minimum version I will do even on hard days is..."

Now attach it to an anchor:

"I will do it right after..."

(waking up, brushing teeth, lunch, finishing work, making coffee, getting into bed)

Now write how you'll track proof:

"I will track it by..."

- ticking a box on a calendar
- a note in your phone
- a dot on a page
- a simple habit tracker

Finally, write this:

"I'm not looking for a breakthrough. I'm building a pattern."

That sentence matters, because it resets your expectations.

Say This to Yourself

If you're tempted to quit because it feels slow, borrow this:

"Slow is still forward."

Or:

"I'm not behind. I'm building."

You Don't Need a Breakthrough – You Need a Practice You Can Keep

If growth feels slower than you expected, good.

That means it's real.

Real growth isn't a performance.

It's a practice.

One you can do on hard days.

One you can repeat.

One that creates evidence.

And evidence is what turns "I hope I can change" into:

"I'm changing."

"Trust thyself: every heart vibrates to that iron string."

— **Ralph Waldo Emerson,** *Self-Reliance* **(1841)**

15

The Quiet Moment You Realise You're Not Second-Guessing Everything

Self-trust is not the same as confidence. Confidence is about outcomes. Self-trust is about process — the knowledge that you can navigate what comes, even without guarantees. It is one of the most hard-won aspects of personal strength, and by this point in the work, you've earned the right to start claiming it.

Self-trust doesn't usually come back with fireworks.

It comes back in small, almost boring moments.

You make a decision and you don't spiral afterward.

You say no and you don't spend three days feeling guilty.

You notice a red flag and you don't talk yourself out of it.

You rest and you don't punish yourself for it.

You feel something and you don't argue with your own feelings like they're a problem to be solved.

And you realise:

You're starting to trust yourself again.

That moment matters more than people realise.

Because trauma doesn't only hurt you.

It can make you doubt your own judgement.

Trauma Can Break Self-Trust (Even If You Look Fine)

A lot of people think the main fallout after trauma is fear.

But one of the sneakiest aftershocks is this:

You stop trusting yourself.

You question your instincts.

You question your decisions.

You question your emotions.

You question your memory.

You question whether you're overreacting.

You question whether you're allowed to want what you want.

And when self-trust is shaky, everything becomes harder.

Because every decision becomes a debate.

Even small ones.

And the debates are exhausting.

Lie #15: "I Can't Trust Myself Until I Feel Confident"

This is the lie people accidentally live by:

"I'll trust myself again when I feel confident."

But confidence is not the starting point.

Confidence is the result.

Confidence is built.

And it's built the same way a bridge is built after an earthquake:

slowly, deliberately, with strong supports.

You don't wait until the bridge feels safe to start building it.

You build your own bridge until it becomes safe.

Self-Trust Isn't a Feeling – It's a Relationship

Here's the reframe:

Self-trust isn't a mood.

It's a relationship you build with yourself.

And like any relationship, it's strengthened the same way:

- honesty
- consistency
- boundaries
- repair after mistakes

- showing up again

If you've lost self-trust, it doesn't mean you're broken.

It means the relationship with yourself has been under strain.

And that relationship can be rebuilt.

Why Self-Trust Gets Shaken

Self-trust can get shaken in a few common ways after trauma.

Sometimes it's because you didn't see it coming.

So your brain concludes, "My judgement is unreliable."

Sometimes it's because you ignored your instincts in the past.

So your brain concludes, "I can't trust myself to protect you."

Sometimes it's because your body reacted intensely—panic, shutdown, numbness.

So your brain concludes, "I can't trust my emotions."

Sometimes it's because people around you minimised or doubted your experience.

So your brain concludes, "Maybe I'm wrong."

And sometimes it's because you had to survive in ways that don't feel like you.

So you conclude, "Maybe I don't even know who I am."

All of that makes sense.

But here's the key:

The conclusion "I can't trust myself" is understandable… and it's not permanent.

The Enemy: The Inner Interrogator

Let's name the enemy in this chapter:

The inner interrogator.

That voice that cross-examines every thought and feeling like you're on trial.

"Are you sure?"

"Are you being dramatic?"

"What if you're wrong?"

"What if you make the wrong choice?"

"What if you regret it?"

"What if you trust the wrong person again?"

"What if you're just broken?"

The inner interrogator often thinks it's protecting you.

But it doesn't protect you.

The inner interrogator paralyses you.

And it keeps you stuck in your head instead of living your life.

Rebuild Self-Trust With Small Proof

Here's the plan for this chapter:

Step 1: Stop demanding certainty

Certainty is a trap. It's not required for self-trust.

Step 2: Make small promises and keep them

Self-trust is built through kept agreements with yourself.

Step 3: Learn to repair after setbacks

Because you will have setbacks. Repair is the difference between growth and shame.

Step 4: Practise listening to your signals

Your body, emotions, and instincts are not enemies. They're information.

That's it.

Small proof, stacked over time.

Try This Today: The Self-Trust Ladder (10 Minutes)

Grab a pen and write:

"If I trusted myself 10% more, I would..."

Now write a list of small actions. Not huge changes. Small ones.

Examples:

- go to bed when I say I will
- take a walk when I feel spun out

- message one safe person instead of isolating
- stop explaining myself to someone unsafe
- eat a real meal instead of running on adrenaline
- book the appointment I keep avoiding
- take a break without justifying it
- make one decision and let it stand

Now choose one and make it tiny.

Write:

"The smallest version of that is..."

Then do it within 24 hours.

That's a rung on the ladder.

And rungs are how you climb.

The Two Skills That Build Self-Trust Fastest

1) Kept promises (even tiny ones)

Self-trust is not built by giant motivational moments.

It's built when you say:

"I'm going to do this small thing."

...and then you do it.

That's the moment your brain starts updating its belief:

"Okay. I can rely on me."

Start ridiculously small if you need to.

You're not trying to impress anyone.

You're trying to rebuild a relationship.

2) Clean repair after setbacks

Setbacks don't destroy self-trust.

Shame does.

Shame says:

"You failed. That proves you can't trust yourself. What's the point?"

Repair says:

"Okay. That happened. What do you need? What's the next step?"

If you want a simple repair script, use this:

1. Name it: "I slipped today."
2. Normalise it: "That's part of rebuilding."
3. Next step: "The smallest stabilising thing I can do now is ____."
4. Kindness: "I'm still on my side."

That is self-trust in action.

Not perfection. Repair.

The Boundary Part of Self-Trust

This matters more than people realise:

Self-trust grows when you stop betraying yourself to keep other people comfortable.

If you keep saying yes when you mean no…

If you keep staying quiet when you need to speak…

If you keep tolerating things that hurt you…

If you keep letting people cross lines…

…your system notices.

And your system concludes:

"I'm not safe with me."

So one of the fastest ways to rebuild self-trust is to practise small boundaries.

Not dramatic. Not aggressive. Just clean.

Try:

"I'm not available for that."

"I'm going to think about it and get back to you."

"That doesn't work for me."

"I'm not discussing this today."

Boundaries are not walls.

They're self-respect in behaviour form.

What Becomes Possible When You Start Trusting Yourself Again

When self-trust returns—even 10% more self-trust—you start noticing big shifts.

You make decisions faster.

You recover from mistakes quicker.

You stop needing everyone to agree with you.

You feel more grounded in your body.

You take steps without needing to feel ready first.

And here's the big one:

You stop treating your life like a courtroom.

You start treating it like a build.

That's where growth becomes durable.

Because durable growth doesn't come from hype.

It comes from self-trust.

Say This to Yourself

If the inner interrogator shows up, borrow this:

"I don't need certainty. I need one decision I can live with."

Or:

"I build self-trust by keeping small promises."

You're Not Here to Get It Perfect – You're Here to Become Reliable to Yourself

You don't rebuild self-trust by never struggling.

You rebuild it by staying on your own side while you struggle.

Tiny promises. Kept consistently.

Clean repair after setbacks.

Small boundaries that protect your energy.

That's how you become someone you can rely on again.

And when you can rely on you, the whole rebuild gets easier.

Because you stop asking, "Can I handle life?"

And you start proving, "I can."

"We tell ourselves stories in order to live."

— **Joan Didion,** *The White Album* **(1979)**

16

The Story You Tell Yourself Becomes the Room You Live In

The question "why did this happen to me?" is one most people eventually stop trying to answer. The more useful question — the one Post-Traumatic Growth research consistently points toward — is "what meaning am I going to make of it?" This chapter is about the difference between those two questions, and why only one of them is worth your energy.

Most people don't realise they're living inside a story.

They think they're living inside facts.

But after trauma, the facts are only one part of the experience.

The other part is the meaning your mind attaches to those facts.

And that meaning becomes a story.

A story you repeat.

A story you defend.

A story you quietly organise your life around.

Which means—without meaning to—you can end up building your future inside a story that was written in your worst moment.

Your Pain Writes a Story for You (If You Don't Write One on Purpose)

After something hard, your mind does what minds do:

It tries to explain.

Your mind tries to make sense of what happened.

It tries to predict what might happen again.

It tries to protect you from risk, disappointment, and danger.

So your mind starts drafting a narrative.

And if you don't choose your story intentionally, trauma will choose one for you.

Not because trauma is clever.

Because trauma is loud.

And the loudest voice often becomes the author.

Lie #16: "This Is Just the Way I Am Now"

This is one of the most dangerous lies, because it sounds like acceptance.

"This is just the way I am now."

Sometimes it shows up as:

- "I'm broken."
- "I can't handle life."
- "I'll never trust anyone again."

- "Nothing is safe."
- "Bad things always happen to me."
- "I'm behind everyone else."
- "I peaked before this happened."

These sentences might feel true in the moment.

But if you turn a moment into an identity, you don't just describe your life...

You shape it.

You Can Tell the Truth Without Trapping Yourself

Let's be clear:

We are not doing fake positivity.

We are not pretending the trauma was good.

We are not rewriting reality.

We're doing something more powerful than that:

We're telling the truth without trapping you inside it.

There's a difference between:

- "This happened, and it hurt me."

and

- "This happened, and now my life is over."

The first is truth.

The second is a conclusion.

And conclusions can be changed.

Your Brain Builds Meaning to Create Safety

A story is not just a story.

A story is a safety strategy.

If your mind can explain what happened, it feels less random.

If it feels less random, it feels more predictable.

If it feels more predictable, your nervous system calms down.

So when your brain tells a bleak story, it's often doing it for a reason:

Bleak stories try to prevent disappointment.

If you expect the worst, you won't be blindsided again.

That strategy makes sense.

It just comes with a cost:

A life that gets smaller.

The Enemy: The Broken Story

Let's name the enemy in this chapter:

The broken story.

You've met this enemy before — back in Chapter 6, when your foundations cracked and your brain rushed to write an explanation. This is where we take the pen back.

The broken story is the version of your narrative where trauma becomes your identity and your future becomes a closed door.

It sounds like:

- "I'm damaged goods."
- "I can't be helped."
- "People can't be trusted."
- "Nothing changes."
- "This is the end of me."

The broken story doesn't always show up as dramatic despair.

Sometimes it shows up as a quiet resignation.

And resignation is how people stop rebuilding.

Shift the Story Without Lying

Here's the plan for this chapter:

Step 1: Catch the story you're living in

Because you can't change what you can't see.

Step 2: Separate facts from conclusions

Facts keep you grounded. Conclusions can imprison you.

Step 3: Rewrite the story into a rebuilding story

Not a "happy" story. A workable one.

Step 4: Prove the new story with one next step

Because stories become believable when behaviour backs them up.

That's it.

No hype.

Truth, structure, evidence.

The Two Stories That Decide Your Direction

Most people end up living in one of these two story types after trauma:

The Broken Story

- "Something happened."
- "It means I'm broken."
- "My life is smaller now."
- "I'll avoid risk to stay safe."
- "I'll wait until I feel ready."
- "I'll keep my real self hidden."

The Rebuilding Story

- "Something happened."
- "It changed me."
- "I'm rebuilding."
- "I'll take small steady steps."

- "I'll practise repair after setbacks."
- "I'll build a life that fits now."

Notice something:

Both stories include the truth that something happened.

The difference is what you do next.

Try This Today: The Story Audit (10 Minutes)

Grab a pen and write three headings:

1) The facts

2) The conclusion I've been living with

3) The rebuilding version

Now fill it in.

1) The facts (no drama, just reality)

What happened and what has changed:

____

____

2) The conclusion I've been living with

This usually starts with "That means…"

____

____

3) The rebuilding version (truth + agency)

This is not "everything is fine."

This is "I'm rebuilding."

Here are examples of rebuilding versions:

- "This hurt me, and I can still heal in layers."
- "I don't trust easily now, and I can learn to trust wisely."
- "I feel behind, and I can still move forward."
- "I lost something important, and I can still build meaning."
- "I'm not who I was, and I'm not finished."

Now write one sentence underneath:

"If this rebuilding story was true, the next step would be…"

Do the smallest version in the next 24 hours.

That's how a story becomes real.

Why This Works: Your Brain Needs Evidence, Not Poetry

A new story won't feel believable at first.

That's normal.

Especially if you've lived in the broken story for a while.

Your brain will say:

"Nice words. Prove it."

So you don't argue with your brain.

You give it evidence.

One step.

One repaired setback.

One boundary.

One safe conversation.

One steady practice.

Stories become believable when they're lived.

Turning Your Trauma Into Your Identity

This matters, so I'll say it plainly:

Your trauma is part of your story.

It is not your entire identity.

If you build your entire identity around the worst thing that happened, you'll feel loyal to your pain—like letting go means betraying the truth.

But letting go of the broken story isn't betrayal.

It's growth.

It's choosing to tell the truth without making your future smaller.

Say This to Yourself

If you catch yourself trapped in the broken story, borrow this:

"This happened. It hurt me. I'm still here."

Or, if you need it shorter:

"Not broken. Rebuilding."

You Are Not the Worst Thing That Happened to You

You are not the worst day of your life.

You are not the moment you fell apart.

You are not your symptoms.

You are not your fear.

You are the person who is still here.

And the fact you're still here means something important:

The story isn't finished.

So let's write it on purpose.

One next step at a time.

"Live the questions now."

— **Rainer Maria Rilke,** *Letters to a Young Poet* **(1903)**

17

The Fastest Way to Ruin Meaning Is to Force It

Not everyone who comes through serious trauma discovers a dramatically different life. But most people find that what they want has shifted. This chapter is about New Possibilities: not as optimism, but as a serious recalibration of what you're actually building toward.

There's a certain kind of comment people make after something hard that can feel cruel, even when it's meant kindly.

"You'll find the lesson."

"Everything happens for a reason."

"This will make you stronger."

"One day you'll be grateful."

And maybe—eventually—some of those statements will land in a way that feels true.

But if they're said too early, or if you say them to yourself too soon, these statements can do damage.

Because forcing meaning too soon can feel like you're denying your own pain.

It can feel like you're trying to tidy up something that is still bleeding.

So let's do this properly.

Meaning, without pressure.

You Think You're Supposed to "Make It Worth It"

A lot of people carry a secret pressure after trauma:

"I have to make this worth something."

As if the only way to justify what happened is to extract a lesson big enough to balance the scales.

But trauma doesn't come with a refund policy.

You don't earn back what you lost by being inspirational.

You don't owe anyone a redemption arc.

And you definitely don't owe the universe a neat moral.

That pressure doesn't create meaning.

It creates performance.

And performance is not the same as healing.

Lie #17: "If I Can't Find Meaning, I'm Doing This Wrong"

This is the lie that turns meaning into another deadline:

"If I can't find meaning, I'm doing this wrong."

But meaning is not a task you complete.

Meaning is something that often emerges over time—especially when you've stabilised, when you've rebuilt some safety, and when your nervous system isn't in constant emergency mode.

So if you're not ready for meaning yet, that doesn't mean you're failing.

It means you're early in the process.

Or it means you're human.

Or both.

Meaning Is Not a Reason – Meaning Is a Direction

This distinction changes everything:

Meaning is not a reason.

Meaning is a direction.

A reason tries to explain why the trauma happened.

A direction asks:

"Given that it happened, how do I want to live now?"

That's a completely different question.

And it doesn't require you to like what happened.

This question requires you to choose what you do with your life moving forward.

People Make Meaning in Different Ways

Some people make meaning through spirituality.

Some people make meaning through service.

Some people make meaning through relationships.

Some people make meaning through new boundaries.

Some people make meaning by becoming the person they wish they'd had back then.

Some people make meaning by telling the truth.

Some people make meaning by rebuilding a life that fits, even if it's quieter than before.

And some people don't make meaning in a deep, philosophical way at all.

They make meaning in the simplest form:

They decide not to let the trauma be the end of them.

That counts.

The Enemy: Spiritual Bypassing and Toxic Meaning

Let's name two enemies here, because they look like growth but often block it.

1) Spiritual bypassing

This is when you use meaning to avoid feelings.

It sounds like:

- "I'm fine. It's all part of the plan."
- "I'm grateful, so I shouldn't feel angry."
- "This is a gift, so I shouldn't be sad."

But if meaning is used to silence grief, it isn't meaning.

It's avoidance wearing a halo.

2) Toxic meaning

This is when you force an interpretation that doesn't fit.

Like telling yourself you're supposed to be happy about what happened.

If the meaning requires you to betray your truth, it will collapse later.

Because your nervous system knows when you're lying.

So we don't do forced meaning.

We do honest meaning.

Let Meaning Emerge, Then Choose a Direction

Here's the plan for this chapter:

Step 1: Stop demanding a reason

Because reasons are often unavailable.

Step 2: Stabilise first

Meaning is hard to access when your system is in survival mode.

Step 3: Ask direction-based questions

Questions that create movement.

Step 4: Choose one value-led action

Because meaning becomes real through behaviour.

That's it.

Not a dramatic life reinvention.

A direction.

Try This Today: Meaning Without Pressure (10 Minutes)

Grab a pen and write:

"I don't need a reason. I need a direction."

Now answer these questions in short sentences:

1. **What do I know matters more to me now than it did before?**

---

2. What do I care less about now?

---

3. What kind of person do I want to be because of this—without pretending I'm glad it happened?

---

4. What is one small action I can take this week that aligns with that person?

Now do the smallest version.

This is how meaning becomes lived, not theorised.

The Two-Handed Truth: Pain and Purpose Can Coexist

There's a mature kind of meaning-making that doesn't deny anything.

It holds two truths at once:

- This hurt me.
- I can still live with intention.
- I didn't choose this.
- I can choose what happens next.
- I wish it never happened.
- I refuse to let it define the rest of my life.

That's not a contradiction.

That's integration.

Integration is where growth lives.

What Meaning Is Not

Let's make this very clear, because it frees people:

Meaning is not:

- proving you're strong
- being inspirational
- convincing other people you're fine
- turning your trauma into a brand
- forcing forgiveness
- forcing gratitude
- pretending everything worked out perfectly

Meaning is not a performance.

Meaning is alignment.

Say This to Yourself

If you feel pressure to find a lesson, borrow this:

"I don't need to make this 'worth it.' I just need to keep rebuilding."

Or:

"Meaning can wait. My next step can't."

You Don't Owe Anyone a Lesson – You Owe Yourself a Life

You don't have to find meaning on demand.

You don't have to turn pain into a neat story.

You don't have to answer the universe.

But you do get to choose a direction.

A direction built on truth.

A direction that honours what happened without worshipping it.

A direction that makes your life larger again.

Meaning doesn't have to be forced.

It can be lived.

One small, honest step at a time.

"How we spend our days is, of course, how we spend our lives."

— Annie Dillard, The Writing Life (1989)

18

The Day You Realise You've Been Functioning, But Not Living

Appreciation of Life is among the most frequently reported Post-Traumatic Growth outcomes — and the most frequently misunderstood. It is not gratitude for what happened. It is a recalibration of attention: what gets noticed, what registers as enough, what no longer needs to be chased.

There's a moment that comes for a lot of people—usually without warning—where you catch yourself and think:

"I've been doing life… but I haven't been *in* it."

You've been coping.

Managing.

Getting through.

Ticking boxes.

Saying the right things.

Holding it together.

From the outside, you might look fine.

But on the inside, it can feel like you're living behind glass.

You're present… but not fully.

And when that realisation hits, it can feel scary.

Because you're not just tired.

You're hungry for your life again.

Survival Mode Becomes Your Default

Survival mode is useful for emergencies.

But trauma can turn it into a lifestyle.

In survival mode, your brain is focused on:

- avoiding danger
- reducing discomfort
- preventing disappointment
- controlling outcomes
- getting through the day

So you start living in a narrow lane.

You do what's necessary.

You don't do what's meaningful.

You get through.

You don't expand.

And over time, you might start believing:

"This is just adulthood."

"This is just what life is now."

"This is as good as it gets."

But that isn't life.

That's endurance.

And endurance is not meant to be permanent.

Lie #18: "If I Start Living Again, Something Bad Will Happen"

This lie doesn't always show up as a sentence. Sometimes it shows up as a feeling.

A nervousness when things start going well.

A suspicion of calm.

A fear of joy.

A sense that if you relax, you'll be blindsided again.

So you stay braced.

Because bracing feels like control.

It feels like protection.

But here's the truth:

Bracing doesn't prevent pain.

It just prevents living.

Living Again Starts Small – It's About Re-Engagement

When people imagine living again, they often picture something dramatic:

A huge goal. A big life change. A new identity. A bold reinvention.

But the shift from surviving to living is usually much smaller and more practical than that.

Living again is not a grand gesture.

It's re-engagement.

It's doing one thing that makes you feel like you're back in your life.

One thing that says, "I'm here."

One thing that's not just coping.

You're Rebuilding Your Capacity for Joy

Joy after trauma can feel unfamiliar.

Not because you don't deserve it.

Because your system learned that safety is temporary.

So when joy shows up, your brain can respond with:

"Careful."

"Don't get ahead of yourself."

"Don't get too comfortable."

"Don't trust this."

This is why some people feel anxious when things start improving.

It's not because they love suffering.

It's because their system is adjusting.

So we don't force joy.

We rebuild capacity for it.

And capacity is built the same way everything else is built in this book:

small, steady steps.

The Enemy: Shrinking Your Life to Feel Safe

Let's name the enemy:

Life shrinking.

It often happens quietly.

You stop going places.

You stop doing things you used to enjoy.

You stop reaching out.

You stop trying new possibilities.

You stop saying yes to the good things.

You stop planning because planning feels risky.

And the world gets smaller.

The tragedy is: it feels safer in the short term.

But in the long term, shrinking your life becomes its own kind of pain.

Because you weren't built only to survive.

You were built to live.

Expand Your Life Without Overwhelming Yourself

Here's the plan for Chapter 18:

Step 1: Identify what *living* looks like for you now

Not what it used to look like. What it looks like now.

Step 2: Choose one "re-engagement" action

One.

Step 3: Make it small enough to succeed

Minimum version.

Step 4: Repeat it until your system trusts it

Because repetition teaches safety.

That's how you go from surviving to living—without pressure.

Try This Today: The Re-Engagement List (10 Minutes)

Grab a pen and write:

"When I feel like I'm living (not just surviving), I'm usually..."

Now list 10 small things—small enough that you can do them without needing a whole new life.

Examples:

- sitting outside with a coffee
- walking somewhere with no goal
- listening to music you actually like
- cooking something simple
- calling a safe person
- being in nature
- reading two pages
- going to a place you used to enjoy
- doing something creative for 10 minutes
- laughing with someone who gets you

Write your list:

1. ____

2. ____

3. ____

4. ____

5. ____

6. ____

7. ____

8. ____

9. ____

10. ____

Now circle **one** and write:

"The minimum version of this is…"

____

Then schedule it.

Not.

A day and time.

Because surviving lives in vagueness.

Living resides in intention.

The "Yes Ladder": How to Say Yes Again Without Panicking

If saying yes feels scary, use what I call a yes ladder.

You don't jump from "no life" to "full life."

You climb.

- Step 1: say yes to something that takes 5 minutes
- Step 2: yes to something that takes 20 minutes
- Step 3: yes to something that involves a person
- Step 4: yes to something that involves a place
- Step 5: yes to something that involves a bit of vulnerability

You climb slowly.

And every yes becomes evidence.

Evidence reduces fear.

Fear reduction increases capacity.

Capacity makes living possible.

Say This to Yourself

If you feel guilty for wanting to live again, borrow this:

"I'm allowed to have a life again."

Or:

"Living doesn't erase what happened. It honours that I survived it."

You Don't Need a Big Life – You Need Your Life

You don't have to reinvent yourself overnight.

You don't have to chase happiness like it's a job.

But you do get to re-enter your life.

One small yes at a time.

One re-engagement moment at a time.

From surviving… to living.

That's not a finish line.

That's a return.

A return to being here.

"All sorrows can be borne if you put them into a story or tell a story about them."

— Isak Dinesen

19

When the Story Stops Dragging You

At some point, the work stops being about managing the aftermath and starts being about integration — weaving what happened into the fabric of who you are. Post-Traumatic Growth researchers describe this as existential change: a revised understanding of what your life is for. This chapter is about arriving there.

There's a moment—usually after a lot of quiet work—where you notice something unexpected.

You think about what happened…

…and it doesn't flatten you the way it used to.

You remember it, and you still feel something, because you're human.

But it's not a full-body takeover.

It's not a spiral.

It's not an identity crisis.

It's a memory.

A chapter.

Not the whole book.

That moment is what integration feels like.

Not forgetting.

Not pretending.

Not getting over it.

Just integration.

You Either Try to Bury It or You Get Stuck Living Inside It

After trauma, people often swing between two extremes.

Extreme one: Bury it

Move on.

Stay busy.

Don't think about it.

Be positive.

Just get on with it.

Extreme two: Live inside it

Replay it.

Analyse it.

Define yourself by it.

Make every decision through it.

Expect danger everywhere.

Neither extreme is freedom.

Burying doesn't resolve it.

Living inside it doesn't release it.

Integration is the middle path.

Lie #19: "If I Still Feel Something, It Means I'm Not Healed"

This lie can keep people chasing a kind of emotional numbness that looks like peace, but isn't.

"If I still feel something, I'm not healed."

But integration doesn't mean you stop feeling.

It means you stop being controlled by what you feel.

It means the memory has a place.

It means you can carry the story without the story carrying you.

Integration Is Not Forgetting – It's Making Space for It

Here's the reframe:

Integration is when the trauma becomes part of your life story without becoming the centre of your life.

It doesn't disappear.

It gets placed.

The trauma becomes something you can hold with maturity.

You can talk about it without collapsing.

You can remember it without losing the present.

You can honour what it cost you without letting it steal everything else.

That's integration.

Your Mind Wants a Safe Place to Store the Memory

When trauma isn't integrated, it tends to pop up in unhelpful ways:

- intrusive thoughts
- body reactions
- mood shifts
- avoidance
- over-control
- emotional numbness
- sudden waves of fear or grief

It's like the memory is still loose in the system.

Integration gives the memory a safe place to live.

Not because you like it.

Because you're tired of being hijacked by it.

The Enemy: Letting Trauma Become the Lens for Everything

When trauma becomes the lens, everything is filtered through it.

Relationships.

Decisions.

Risk.

Joy.

Work.

Future plans.

Your identity.

And then even good things can feel suspicious.

Even calm can feel unsafe.

Even growth can feel risky.

So the work of integration is partly this:

We stop letting the trauma be the only lens.

We widen the lens.

We include other truths.

We allow other chapters.

Integration Doesn't Happen Through a Plan

Integration doesn't happen through a plan. It happens through honest reflection — looking at what has changed, naming it accurately, and deciding what to carry forward.

Take as long as you need with the following two sets of questions. There is no time limit. This is not an exercise. It's a taking-stock.

Looking Back

What is genuinely different now compared to when this began?

What do you know about yourself that you didn't know before?

What have you stopped doing that was costing you?

What did you find out you were capable of?

Looking Forward

What is being built now? Name it as specifically as you can.

What matters more than it used to?

What matters less?

What does the person you're becoming actually look like in daily life?

Try This Today: The Integration Page (10 Minutes)

Grab a pen and write these headings:

1) What happened

One or two sentences. No detail spiral.

2) What it cost me

Name the losses honestly.

3) What I rebuilt

Name the strengths and practices you've built since.

4) What I'm taking forward

Values, priorities, boundaries, ways of living.

5) What I refuse to become because of this

This is powerful because it draws a line.

That page is not meant to solve everything.

It's meant to locate the story.

Camille's Story

Five years after the accident that ended her career as a physiotherapist, Camille was teaching anatomy at a community college. She hadn't planned for it. She'd stumbled into a short-term contract during her recovery, stayed because she turned out to be good at it, and eventually stopped thinking of it as "what she was doing in the meantime."

She still had hard days. She still occasionally felt the particular grief of watching a patient move freely in the way she used to and couldn't anymore. That hadn't disappeared.

But she'd stopped organising her identity around what had been lost, and started organising it around what she was now doing with what she knew. The accident was part of the story. It was not the whole story. The version of Camille who walked into that classroom every week had been shaped by what happened — not despite it, and not because of it, but with it. That's what integration looks like. Not resolution. Incorporation.

The Integration Ritual: A Simple Way to Honour Without Obsessing

Ritual sounds dramatic, but it can be simple.

Here are a few options:

- **A date ritual:** once a year, you do something kind for yourself and acknowledge what you survived.

- **A place ritual:** you visit a place that feels grounding—beach, park, quiet café—and reflect for 10 minutes.
- **A writing ritual:** you write one page titled "What I know now."
- **A service ritual:** you do one act that reflects your values—support someone, volunteer, mentor, give time.
- **A closure ritual:** you write a letter you never send, then safely dispose of it.

Ritual is not about theatre.

It's about containment.

It keeps the memory from leaking everywhere.

It says:

"This has a place. And my whole life isn't that place."

The Truth About Integration: You Don't Integrate Once – You Integrate in Layers

Integration isn't a one-time achievement.

It happens in layers.

You integrate a piece.

Then life reveals a deeper piece.

Then you integrate again.

That doesn't mean you're back at the start.

It means you're processing at a deeper level.

That's what healing looks like when it's real.

Say This to Yourself

If you feel the story pulling you back into the past, borrow this:

"This is part of my story. It is not the whole story."

Or shorter:

"A chapter. Not the book."

You Get to Carry It With Strength, Not With Chains

Integration is not erasing the past.

It's placing it.

Honouring it.

Learning from it.

And then living forward.

You don't have to pretend what happened to you didn't matter.

But you also don't have to give it the final word.

Because you're not the worst thing that happened to you.

You're the person who lived through it… and rebuilt.

And that means the story can be carried—with strength, not with chains.

"No man ever steps in the same river twice."

— Heraclitus (c. 500 BC)

20

You Keep Looking for the Old Life — But It's Not Coming Back

Restoration means putting the pieces back in the same order. Reconstruction means asking which pieces you actually want to keep.

This chapter is about reconstruction. Not restoration. Those two words are doing very different jobs, and by now you may already sense the difference between them. We're going to name this difference clearly — and then talk about what it looks like to keep building.

Which brings us to the only question that matters now — not "How do I get back to who I was?" You've probably stopped asking that one. The question is: Who am I becoming, and is that person someone I can respect?

And here you are at the other end of it.

This is not a book you had to complete perfectly. It's a book you had to move through honestly.

But you're here. You've done the reading, the reflecting, the uncomfortable sitting-with-things. You've taken the next step when you didn't feel ready. You've built the floor — the basic stability that kept you functional on the hard days. You've layered the foundation — the practices that moved you from surviving into something that looks more like living. You've worked through identity, through relationships, through meaning. You've probably argued with some of this. You've probably skipped an exercise or two. That's fine.

You might not have noticed when it shifted. These things rarely announce themselves.

Not because you gave up. Not because you settled. But because somewhere in the middle of all this work, you started to become someone else. Someone shaped by what happened to you, but not broken by it. Someone who carries the weight differently now.

There's a moment — and most people who've been through something serious can name it exactly — when you realise you've stopped waiting to feel like yourself again.

The Difference Between a Good Life and a Small Life

A good life is not a life without pain.

A good life is a life with agency.

A life where your choices reflect your values more often than your fear.

A life where you recover faster after setbacks.

A life where you tell the truth.

A life where you allow connection.

A life where you re-engage.

A life where you take the next step even when you're not okay yet.

A small life is not always sad.

Sometimes a small life looks fine.

But it's built around avoidance, bracing, and waiting.

This book has been an invitation to build something bigger than that.

Not louder.

Bigger.

What You Do When You Have a Bad Week Again

Because you will.

Not because you're failing.

Because you're human.

When you have a bad week:

1. Name it: "This is a wave."
2. Normalise it: "This is part of rebuilding."
3. Minimum toolkit: "Stability first."
4. One next step: "Keep moving."
5. Connection: "Don't do it alone."

That is the rebuild cycle.

Use it forever.

Your Final Exercise

Write one sentence that completes this: "The person I am now — the one who made it through this — is someone who…"

Don't overthink it. Write the first true thing.

What Post-Traumatic Growth Actually Means (In Plain Language)

Let's keep this simple as we close:

Post-traumatic growth doesn't mean you're happy it happened.

It means that in the aftermath, you rebuild in ways that can lead to positive change—often in relationships, strength, possibilities, appreciation, and meaning.

Not because trauma is a gift.

But because you're capable of building a life that is not defined by what hurt you.

Growth isn't the opposite of pain.

Growth is what you do with pain once you've stopped pretending it doesn't exist.

Say This to Yourself

If you need one line to carry forward, let it be this:

"My future isn't a return. It's a building."

Or:

"I'm not okay yet—and I'm still moving."

You don't get to go back.

That's not a tragedy. It's the most honest thing this book can offer you. The version of your life that existed before — the one you might still sometimes reach for — isn't coming back. And the person who lived that version isn't quite who you are anymore either.

But here's what is true: the person standing on the other side of all this work is more capable than you were when you started. More aware. More honest about what matters. More able to tell the difference between what deserves your energy and what doesn't.

That person didn't appear despite what happened. They emerged through it.

Your future isn't a return. It's a build. And you already know how to do that, because you've been doing it the whole time you've been reading this book.

One step. Then another. That's how it's always worked.

The Story Isn't Finished

If you're still here, still reading, still trying—even quietly—that means something.

It means you didn't let the worst chapter become the final chapter.

You're not the person you were.

And you don't have to be.

Because you are building someone new.

Someone steadier.

Someone truer.

Someone more intentional.

Someone more connected.

Someone who knows what matters.

Not because you wanted this journey.

But because you refused to let it be the end of you.

And that's the whole point:

The future isn't a return.

It's a build.

And you're already building it.

Acknowledgements and Selected Sources

Acknowledgements

Thank you to every person who has ever said, "I'm not okay yet," and kept going anyway. Your honesty is the reason this book exists.

Thank you to the researchers and clinicians who have spent decades studying how people can change for the better after adversity, especially Richard G. Tedeschi and Lawrence G. Calhoun, and the wider community of contributors who helped shape the theory, research, and clinical applications of post-traumatic growth.

To Jennifer Tomscha, whose editorial eye sharpened every chapter of this book — including its title.

To Marvin Oka, whose behavioural modelling work planted the seed that grew into my first book — and, in time, into this one.

And to my wife, Christine, and our children — who lived every page of this story before it was a story.

Selected Sources

This book is written for everyday readers, not as an academic text. If you'd like to go deeper into the science behind the ideas, these works are a strong starting point:

- Tedeschi, R. G., Shakespeare-Finch, J., Taku, K., & Calhoun, L. G. (2018). *Posttraumatic Growth: Theory, Research, and Applications.* Routledge.
- Tedeschi, R. G., & Calhoun, L. G. (1995). *Trauma and Transformation: Growing in the Aftermath of Suffering.* Sage.
- Tedeschi, R. G., & Calhoun, L. G. (1996). The Posttraumatic Growth Inventory: Measuring the positive legacy of trauma. *Journal of Traumatic Stress, 9*, 455–471.
- Tedeschi, R. G., & Calhoun, L. G. (2004). Posttraumatic growth: Conceptual foundations and empirical evidence. *Psychological Inquiry, 15*, 1–18.
- Calhoun, L. G., & Tedeschi, R. G. (2006). The foundations of posttraumatic growth: An expanded framework. In *Handbook of Posttraumatic Growth: Research and Practice* (pp. 3–23).
- Calhoun, L. G., & Tedeschi, R. G. (2013). *Posttraumatic Growth in Clinical Practice.* Routledge.
- Tedeschi, R. G., Cann, A., Taku, K., Senol-Durak, E., & Calhoun, L. G. (2017). The posttraumatic growth inventory: A revision integrating existential and spiritual change. *Journal of Traumatic Stress, 30*(1), 11–18.

- Cann, A., Calhoun, L. G., Tedeschi, R. G., Kilmer, R. P., Gil-Rivas, V., Vishnevsky, T., & Danhauer, S. C. (2010). The Core Beliefs Inventory: A brief measure of disruption in the assumptive world. *Anxiety, Stress, & Coping, 23,* 19–34.
- Cann, A., Calhoun, L. G., Tedeschi, R. G., Triplett, K. N., Vishnevsky, T., & Lindstrom, C. M. (2011). Assessing posttraumatic cognitive processes: The Event Related Rumination Inventory. *Anxiety, Stress, & Coping, 24,* 137–156.

Janoff-Bulman, R. (1992). Shattered Assumptions: Towards a New Psychology of Trauma. Free Press.

Frankl, V. E. (2006). Man's Search for Meaning. Beacon Press. (Original work published 1946)

van der Kolk, B. (2014). The Body Keeps the Score: Brain, Mind, and Body in the Healing of Trauma. Viking.

About the Author

Bill Gasiamis knows what it means to have your life split into "before" and "after." Between 2012 and 2014, he survived three brain haemorrhages — an experience that changed not just his health, but his understanding of what recovery, identity, and growth actually look like from the inside.

Rather than treat his survival as a story to move past, Bill built his life's work around it. He is the host of the Recovery After Stroke podcast — more than 400 episodes exploring the psychology, practicalities, and possibilities of life after a major health event, and one of the longest-running podcasts of its kind.

He is the author of *The Unexpected Way That A Stroke Became The Best Thing That Happened: Ten Tools For Recovery And Personal Transformation*, and speaks internationally on post-traumatic growth — helping individuals, organisations, and health professionals understand how people don't just survive serious life events, but sometimes change for the better because of them.

His work sits at the intersection of lived experience and evidence-based research. He is not interested in inspiration for its own sake. He is interested in what actually helps people move

— and in showing people that the size of a life after trauma is not fixed.

Find Bill, the podcast, and every resource mentioned in this book at billgasiamis.com/book